Thomas,

All the best in
your future.

— E. Smith

future, inc.

how businesses can
anticipate and profit
from what's next

ERIC GARLAND

AMACOM AMERICAN MANAGEMENT ASSOCIATION
New York ○ Atlanta ○ Brussels ○ Chicago ○ Mexico City
San Francisco ○ Shanghai ○ Tokyo ○ Toronto ○ Washington, D.C.

This publication is designed to provide accurate and authoritative information in regard to the subject matter covered. It is sold with the understanding that the publisher is not engaged in rendering legal, accounting, or other professional service. If legal advice or other expert assistance is required, the services of a competent professional person should be sought.

Library of Congress Cataloging-in-Publication Data

Garland, Eric
    Future, inc.: how businesses can anticipate and profit from what's next / Eric Garland.
        p. cm.
    Includes index.
    ISBN-13: 978-0-8144-0897-1
    ISBN-10: 0-8144-0897-4

Printing number
10 9 8 7 6 5 4 3 2 1

CONTENTS

FOREWORD

A professor friend, as part of a study comparing American and Japanese innovation practices, was interviewing the CEO of a top-ten firm in Tokyo. Having taken so much of the man's time, he apologized. The CEO replied that there was nothing more important in his work than talking to people about the long-term future. Compare him to the typical Fortune 500 CEO, who is caught up in micromanagement despite claims to the contrary. Find the American CEO who can talk knowingly about the long-term future for two hours without notes; flip charts; or that cursed sham substitute for knowledge, the tedious PowerPoint presentation. This kind of CEO behavior influences those in his or her succession plan, creating an upper echelon immune to concepts and forecasts beyond the product line and the next few years.

How can we overcome the systemic indifference to the mid- and long-term future? Garland's book can be a giant step in that direction. His experience as a consulting futurist and as a business-intelligence specialist serving many kinds of enterprises gives him the qualifications to lay out the reliable description presented in this book about how to study the future. Garland's snappy style and illustrations of how the process works may lure even the mossiest of mossbacks to give it a try.

Garland's approach can accomplish three things. First, it can help people usefully explore the future to influence organizational decision making. Second, it may induce executives to continually think about the future and make it central to planning. Third, it will make people wiser sponsors, buyers, and users of future studies and their claims.

I hope you enjoy *Future, Inc.* as much as I have.

Joseph F. Coates, professional futurist, author of *2025: Scenarios of U.S. and Global Society Reshaped by Science & Technology*

ACKNOWLEDGMENTS

I am tremendously grateful to be able to work as a futurist and to be able to write about it. This is more fun than anyone should be allowed to have at work.

Allow me to thank so many people who made this and many other things possible.

Four men shaped my thinking about business, and I need to recognize them here.

My father, Paul Garland, who brought me up with a Vermont work ethic and the opportunity to lug bags of cow manure around his farm store (and who also taught me to read).

Jeff Washburn, whose Kentucky Fried Chicken taught me more about management, strategy, quality, and customer service than any business school. For real.

Bob Berman, whose humor and business acumen is without peer, and whose endless mockery of fancy management consultants keeps me grounded. He convinced me early that real business is "Buy low, sell high, collect early, pay late. All the rest is window dressing."

Joe Coates, a master futurist and good friend, from whom I have stolen every idea I could possibly write down or remember.

His dining room table—with its endless pot of decaf—has been the location of an invaluable education.

The list of people to whom I owe gratitude is very long indeed. Without Lilly Ghahremani and Stefanie Von Borstel at Full Circle Literary, there would be nothing here to read. Special thanks to Erin Weed, Storm Cunningham, and Veronica Monet for going through the author life with me. Josette Bruffaerts-Thomas for endless faith. The National Capitol Region World Future Society presidents, Lynne Puetz, Alex Graham at Society of Competitive Intelligence Professionals, and Dr. Kirk Larsen at George Washington University—thank you for your input.

Friends and family, you know the story. God bless and thank you.

Finally, this is for my wife, Katherine, the main reason I am excited to look at the future.

today's chaos; tomorrow's opportunity

A funny thing happened in the music industry a few years ago. Record companies began suing their customers. The Record Industry Association of America filed lawsuits against, among other defendants, 13-year-old girls in order to stem the rising tide of Internet downloading of MP3 files. Most would agree that lawsuits are a less than perfect way to relate to people who buy your products, especially since the industry normally spends millions to attract teenagers. Why the record companies made this peculiar choice illustrates why, in this rapidly changing world, foresight is so essential.

When you look back to the 1990s, it is important to recognize that record executives are not stupid. The marketing and strategic planners at companies like Sony, Atlantic, and Universal were and continue to be experts in finding talent, market segmentation, retail channels, branding, and promotion—all the things you need to compete in the entertainment industry. They were right on top of their competitors, scanning their marketplace for new trends in customer taste, tracking the moves of other record companies, and even looking out for substitute products. Video games and cable television were as much potential competitors as another record label with a hot band. These executives did what most people do—they looked at their competition and their customers and tried to anticipate the next move.

What they did not follow were a couple of key technological trends *outside* of their industry. Throughout the 1990s, home computer ownership was increasing. At the same time, more and more computers were capable of accessing the Internet, which was seen by most as just a communications protocol, invented by the Department of Defense. Sure, it was useful for scientific researchers and the very, very geeky, but of what possible use could it be to the home user?

At first, the proliferation of Web-connected computers wasn't even on the radar of most music industry executives—it certainly didn't scare them. From 1995 to 1999, most connections were at dial-up speed, 56k per second, a speed so slow that it could have no impact on their business. Yes, record companies could use Web pages to put up rosters of bands, replete with low-quality samples that gave the computer user a little taste of what a full CD would deliver at much higher quality. The Internet was a neat tool for marketing new bands, getting a little publicity through a new media. That was it.

Were they wrong? The story was hardly over.

Broadband connections were offered in more locations at reasonable prices consumers could afford. On the horizon were new improvements in software that enabled audio to be compressed into a small amount of data while retaining good sound quality. The file format called MP3, or "Motion Picture Engineering Group Audio Layer 3," was born. Unlike previous attempts to digitize music into a small package, MP3 actually sounded like music. Unlike copying music onto cassette tapes, you could make an unlimited number of copies at the touch of a button. This technical revolution occurred at the exact moment that consumers everywhere were connecting to the Internet at home or at work.

All hell broke loose.

If you recognize the word "Napster," then you remember the chaos that resulted. By late 1999 and 2000, free music poured out of the Internet with no cost to consumers and few technical difficulties. Napster was so terrifyingly efficient at connecting consumers with one another to "share" their music that anyone with a computer could find any song in moments with a simple Web search. It was like going shopping for free. You entered the name of the song you wanted; Napster found another user who had that song, and, within minutes, the other computer "shared" it with you. Music sales figures soon showed the impact. Music no longer was a physical product, made of plastic; it was now an ethereal concept that could be stored on a hard drive and shared at will, broadcast to anyone with a few moments to do a Web search.

Moreover, market research showed that young people trading MP3 files had significantly different values than their elders when it came to the legality and morality of downloading. Appeals to younger consumers by RIAA (Recording Industry Association of America) to equate the trading of MP3 with shoplifting fell flat. After all, people have been sharing tapes of their favorite tunes since the arrival of the cassette tape over forty years ago. The difference, however, was enormous. Now, you could share your music with millions of people.

In America, when all else fails, you sue. The industry did just that, tracking the IP addresses of some file downloaders to reveal their identities and then serving them with lawsuits. The lawsuits usually resulted in small fines, but the industry's reputation suffered. The whole episode made record companies look like bullies, who were taking out their business woes on consumers.

To think, if industry executives had spent a little more time thinking about how technologies could affect their business, we might have had iTunes five years earlier (and fewer teenagers hiring attorneys to defend themselves from record labels)!

The Transformative Power of Trends

Welcome to the future, where trends combine and interact in unheard of ways to present your business with wild and unprecedented threats and opportunities. In today's world, you don't need to think about just your future, but about the future of nearly everything. Now, if you are a record company you aren't just worried about other entertainment providers; you've got to be looking at electronics in the home and computers in the workplace and the next technological innovation to see tomorrow's competitive challenge.

Today, the MP3 business case seems bizarre. How else can we explain the fact that otherwise competent executives were flailing about, demonizing their own customers because they were left, in their minds, with few or no options? They were presented not with just one trend, home computers, but several trends all at once—combined with a new generation who thought very differently about their product. Within just a few years, the entire business model turned from manufacturing a physical product to providing a service. Sure, now we have iTunes, MusicMatch, and other services, but the industry has had to shift from a paradigm of pushing plastic around the country, to selling ring tones to cell phone users. It has been anything but easy.

Like the record industry fifteen years ago, businesses today are facing a special kind of challenge. They aren't just dealing with traditional threats from new competitors, substitute products, and shifts in the market, but are instead seeing entire industries turned on their heads in incredibly short periods. This significantly more difficult phenomenon occurs when too many changes occur at one time and, in effect, begin to fold in on one another. This is what I call *superconnection*, the interaction of multiple forces in society and technology at one time. Of course, there have been disruptive technologies and social trends in the past, but today, things are accelerating so rapidly, and globalization spreads change so quickly it's as if it were all happening in your backyard.

Today, the sciences have begun to overlap as biotechnology, chemistry, and physics advance to become nanotechnology. Globalization meets new information technology, and your customer service reps suddenly speak with a foreign accent. Your biggest market segment is suddenly retired people, because the Baby Boomers are aging. India's middle class is nearly as big as the population of Europe. Traditional competitors fade; completely new ones appear. Your own customers become as big a threat as your fiercest rival. Companies in countries you've never heard of begin outproducing your factories. Chaos seems to reign.

Welcome to your new world. It may seem overwhelming, but you have options.

Getting a Jump on the Future

Chaos is not impossible to manage, but it is tough to do it very quickly. The only way to manage this period of hyperactive change is to look ahead, to study the potential changes implied by what you see on the horizon. It can be done, if you give your-self enough time to look at external forces before the problem lands in your lap.

Take, for example, a famous global company like Nokia. You may have one of its cell phones in your pocket right now. Electronics aren't that company's first product, by any means. Founded in 1865, Nokia was really a rubber boot manufacturer, heavily invested in the pulp and paper industry, a company that saw massive turbulence ahead and made a dash for the future. Because it worked, you have that distinctive ring emanating from your purse or pocket.

In the 1980s, Nokia CEO Jorma Ollila faced a knotty strate-gic problem looming in the near-term. It was likely that one of its biggest customers, the Soviet Union, was going out of business.

With foresight, Nokia was able to transform itself. Ollila knew that the social and technological changes on the horizon were going to decimate the company if he did not act. Nokia's businesses were about to face fierce competition and one of its top customers was disappearing. As in any large, unwieldy cor-poration, Nokia needed as much time as possible to prepare for the future. Ollila looked ahead to a world transformed by both technology and the end of the Cold War and made a calculated gamble. He scanned the trends on the horizon and saw new opportunities in telecom unleashed by the existence of small, more powerful microprocessors and an explosion in global com-merce due to the end of U.S./Soviet tensions.

With this understanding, Ollila pushed the company to focus on just one industry—telecommunications, specifically wireless telephony. It was bold and risky. The company had expanded into cable and rubber back in the 1920s and further expanded into electronics in the 1950s. In fact, Nokia began producing mobile phones in the 1970s and 1980s, but under the visionary leadership of Ollila, after 1991, Nokia sold off the majority of its other businesses and bet the company on microprocessor-based cellular phones. They caught the wave, and Nokia moved to the forefront of the expansion of the mobile telephony market. Despite potential bankruptcy, Nokia became a world-beating business whose revenue is as big as the entire government of Finland. Nokia accepted the challenge of transformation and won.

But what if you don't have enough time for a major restructuring? You might see trouble on the horizon, but what could happen if there isn't enough time to react?

Consider Eastman Kodak, once a world leader in photography and imaging and a world-class corporation that made billions from its innovations. It put photography in the hands of consumers, reducing a complex chemical process to a device that anyone could use. Kodak became one of the world's most successful companies, trading on its knowledge of chemical processes and a deep understanding of consumers. Its assets, physical and intellectual, were in chemicals. The end product was imaging, but the factories it owned made chemical film.

What Kodak failed to appreciate was how fast the digital revolution would make chemical film a technology of the past. Kodak's competitive advantage was decidedly not in computer chips, memory, and software, but the photography industry moved to a digital world in a matter of years. Large chemical factories grew irrelevant as cameras became digital, eschewing the need for film. As more imaging products became digital, Kodak continued to lose revenue and profits in the segment that first brought it to prominence, film and imaging systems.

Kodak, in the eyes of many analysts, is flailing. Perhaps not to the point of suing teenagers, but not exactly mastering the future. Its most recent annual report sounds understandably nervous as it explains its dollar-per-share loss. Kodak acknowledges that digital imaging is eating its lunch, but tries to reassure the investor by mentioning that movies are still being made on film, and that every Oscar-winning movie since 1928 has been shot on Kodak film.

What Kodak is omitting or ignoring is the fact that digital cameras are becoming higher quality every year. Even filmmakers like George Lucas have publicly said they cannot wait until digital cameras are good enough to cut film out of the entire process, so they can just e-mail the digital movie to the cinema and show it with digital projection as well. Once digital filmmaking is of similar quality to traditional film, you can bet that Hollywood will not feel as nostalgic as Kodak's investor relations people will about their old technology.

Now, interestingly, Kodak's position differs a bit from the music industry's, in terms of its awareness of the bad stuff around the corner. Record executives had their heads entirely in the sand. The executives at Kodak were saying as far back as the late 1990s that they knew a revolution was coming, but they weren't sure how to turn the ship around in time.

The contrast of Nokia and Kodak illustrates perfectly how the future affects business. New competitors, product substitutions, and changes in the market are not new. But the speed and complexity of these changes are giving leaders whiplash. One minute, you are the world's leading innovator in photography; the next you wish you had a division that made computer chips, because the future just got gloomy. One minute, you are selling records; the next you are deposing little Brittany Johnson from down the street for swapping MP3s with her friends. The next moment, you call a board meeting because the Soviet Union collapsed and you're going to start making cell phones instead of stationery. What the hell is going on here, if you don't mind me asking?

Many leaders—from local economic development boards to investors to the executive suite—are asking that question. The changes are circling around us, popping up in the headlines and appearing in the form of new realities in our businesses. Italy is getting old, just like Japan, Russia, the United States, and most Western nations. Biotechnology is getting cheap. Nobody has a solution for the addiction to oil. The ethnic face of France is changing. China has too many boys. The rich-poor gap is increasing. It is interesting to read about—but leading an organization in the face of this seems daunting at the very least.

The Future and *Your* Future

This brings us to the subject of you. Whether you are running a corporation, making government policy, or starting a small business out of your garage, you are probably confused, amazed, and overwhelmed by all the potential changes promised by the future. Perhaps you are asking yourself, "Will I end up like Nokia, mastering the future by seeing new opportunities before others do and acting on them, or will I end up like the record industry and Kodak, out of time, faced with terrible options?"

You may have less drastic reasons than they did for needing or wanting to know what is next. Not every industry is facing such dramatic changes forcing life-or-death decisions. Maybe you run a bowling alley and just want to know what the customer of the future will want for entertainment. Maybe you are considering a second career and wonder what jobs will be hot in the next few years. You could be an investor trying to get in early to profit from what the future holds. Instead of focusing on today or feeling overwhelmed by the future, isn't it better to know how to interpret this crazy world and come out on top?

Of course it is, and I have just the thing to help you do it.

PART 1

Tools and Techniques

YOU WANT TO know about the future. I've never met you, but I know one thing about you. It's the one trait that unites all humans—Pentagon planners, pharmaceutical executives, soccer moms, kids, and farmers: Each of us wishes we could see into the future. You want to know what will go right. You want to know what will be a disaster. You would like to be surprised. From the Oracle at Mt. Olympus to Nostradamus to stock market analysts—everybody tries to get a look ahead.

That's fantasy, of course! We all know you can't tell the future. It's impossibly complex, so we must all wait and see; at least, that's what conventional wisdom tells us. Conventional wisdom is partly right. You cannot know for certain what *specific* events are going to take place at precise times.

There is, however, most certainly a way to:

○ Understand the trends that will change your life

○ Evaluate the best forecasts from experts in their fields

○ Put these together in compelling scenarios depicting multiple ways the world might look

in order to:

○ Decide what these possibilities could mean for you

and

○ Educate others on the potential choices that will be available

This is far from clairvoyance, but it is a very useful skill, especially for the modern leader. At least that's what hundreds of major corporations and government agencies have thought for years when they've commissioned *professional studies of the future* to improve their thinking and their leadership of major institutions that affect the lives of millions.

What is more important is that you too can use these skills on a daily basis. Futures studies do not rely on clairvoyance, but rather on a simple method of collecting information, analyzing it with the future in mind, and telling the stories in your organization. In the first part of *Future, Inc.* you will learn what these tools are and how to use them.

It takes faith to look into the future. Many people are intimidated by the vast amount of change they have to manage. This is not work for the meek! I congratulate you on your decision, and I look forward to going on this journey with you.

futurism

the antidote
to chaos

Y es, the world is changing quickly, with its promise of chaos and opportunity. It may seem overwhelming, but I have good news for you. Understanding the future, as it affects your decisions, can become an everyday part of the way you think. You don't need a Rolodex of experts on speed dial to interpret everything for you. Anyone can know more about the future. You may never become a professional futurist, but everyone can be vigilant about the major changes coming for our businesses, our governments, even our families.

Forget the jokes about the tea leaves, wizard hats, crystal balls, and ESP. Predicting the future has nothing to do with them and everything to do with curiosity about the world around you. To know more about what is coming, simply follow what is happening in different industries. Exploring the future is about finding a few trends that could change your world and keeping an eye on them on a regular basis. Futuring is about paying attention to both society and technology and asking yourself: "Yes, but what will this mean in five years? What about ten years?" These simple acts change the way we think about the future, such as whether to sell a small business and retire in a decade, or build three new factories in Bangladesh that will take six years to become profitable.

You are about to discover the tools that will help you take all the information you have available to you and turn it into a cogent view of the future. Once you have that vision, you can use it to enhance every decision you make. That way, you won't be making plans believing that film is the future of cinema. You will not miss changes like the MP3 and end up making lamentable decisions. You will see new opportunities before your competitors, just as Nokia did. You will understand your role in a bigger world.

Futurism and Strategic Planning

Professional studies of the future have been part of the executive arsenal for around 40 years. Futurism is the process of discovering what trends will change our world, analyzing their potential impact on specific activities, and then communicating to colleagues what lies ahead. As part of strategic planning or regular collection of business intelligence, futurism has a long history of success.

In 1999, consumer goods companies wanted to know how the future would change packaging. They wanted to know about the soup can and the shampoo bottle of the future. Packaging engineers are regular folks. They live for cardboard boxes, extruded plastic bottles, and aluminum cans. Typically, peanut butter jars are not at the vanguard of the sciences, but, in this instance, there was a lot to learn about the future.

The key was to take a broader view of what packaging meant to consumers around the world. With the help of professional futurists, they tore apart the trends in society and technology. Looking at society, they learned that future packaging designs would really mean something to the developing world, where people reuse bags, boxes, and cans, often for years.

Their study of future technological advances hit pay dirt. They looked at the shrinking size of electronics and realized that soon radio-frequency ID (RFID) tags would be cheap enough to include in packaging. RFID tags are tiny radio devices that send out a few bits of information, like a bar code, to a small area around the package. Looking further ahead, they saw that their biggest customers, Big Box stores like Wal-Mart, were digitizing their operations as much as possible to improve efficiency and reduce inventory loss.

Because of this study, consumer goods companies realized packaging would need to become part of the digital economy— your cans, bottles, and plastic bags would need to be smart! Today, seven years later, you can see IBM capitalizing on this, selling "slap and ship" RFID tags to retailers. These technologies aren't on every box (yet), but these packaging engineers were able to anticipate the needs of their customers years in advance, which gave the industry time to decide what the right technologies would be and when the right time was to launch the new design.

Governments use this kind of thinking in a variety of ways. This scary but potentially real scenario is an example of one such application. Terrorism, unfortunately, is on most people's minds. National governments use futuring to predict the capabilities of the terrorists of tomorrow. They monitor developments in both society and technology to see where terrorists might gain an edge.

Some forecasts show that the cost of biotechnology will fall far enough that smaller groups could afford to obtain the equipment needed to alter bacteria. Futurists working for the federal government envisioned a scenario in which terrorists might one day genetically engineer a bacterium or a virus that would target Ashkenazi Jews (originally from Eastern Europe) or Japanese people, but it could be any group with a distinct genetic makeup. For this reason, agencies constantly monitor the power of biotechnology as well as any terrorist networks that are showing an interest in science. The goal is to limit the terrorists' weaponry to homemade bombs and razor blades instead of genetically engineered plagues. In this way, governments are designing policies for biotechnology that allow scientific progress as well as protection for their citizens.

These are just two examples. Hundreds of organizations use future studies to make sure their strategic plans are on target and to help them design new products and services. Smaller companies can keep abreast of the future to anticipate the needs of the larger companies that make up their customer base.

Futurism is flexible enough to improve planning for all kinds of organizations.

What Understanding the Future Will Do for You

If you are going to spend your valuable time and money studying the future, you should know what you could expect to get from it. Although the specific insights may vary from industry to industry, leaders who study the future gain the following:

A BROADER PERSPECTIVE

In general, people don't have time to consider what is going on in the larger world. Their daily lives are so full that just managing the present is tough enough. They are constantly concerned with the crisis of the day. The larger perspective about where the organization is headed and how the world is changing is often lost. Two years ahead begins to seem like the distant future; even the next quarter could be a completely different world. In addition, as businesses seek more precise niches in order to maintain profitability, we are becoming a world of specialists. This is a good thing when it means we find a competitive, profitable niche. The danger is becoming so focused on our little part of the world that we miss the bigger picture.

A CHALLENGE OF THEIR BASIC ASSUMPTIONS

You already probably know how the future will turn out, right? Come on, you probably have a hunch about what will and will not change, if you are like most people. But when you compare your assumptions with hard data from future-trend research, are they correct? Without a study of the future, you always take the chance that you are harboring dangerous *unexamined assumptions* about the future that could trip you up and cause a strategic misstep as the future changes around you.

Perhaps examining assumptions is not the primary reason people commission or perform a study of the future, but it is one of the most useful side benefits. That's not to say it's comfortable; questioning your assumptions is like yanking your comforter off on a cold winter morning. But that's what futures research is there for. After all, remember, it is *impossible* to know exactly how the future will turn out—and if anyone ever promises that, keep one hand on your wallet. The value of a futures study is to shock you and change your mind—to get the message that records could soon fit in an e-mail—no matter how painful the realization.

The cardinal rule of futurism is *if the findings confirm everything you ever thought about the world and where it is going, it is useless.* You have learned nothing. The true benefits come when your basic assumptions about the future are challenged and explored; only then can you perceive new information about the future and act on it. In addition, because most of us don't discuss the future very often in our daily lives, you may not know what you assume to be true about the future until you talk about it.

For example, back in 2000, while discussing the impact of information technology on construction, an executive from an engineering firm was having real trouble accepting what the job site of the future would look like. Although he could imagine advanced software coordinating megaprojects, he really resisted the idea that the construction worker of 2015 would have the computer skills to run handheld devices that update plans and check out tools securely—advances that would improve efficiency and reduce loss.

The futures study we conducted forecast that construction devices in 2015 would be wireless, simple, tough, and powerful. The construction company would just need to make certain that when a tool is checked out of the shed it leaves a digital trail. The supervisor or construction-site boss would just need to tell the carpenter on the job site that the engineer altered the plans and moved the staircase two feet to the right. Today, Bluetooth wireless communications, Java software, and the IPv6 Internet protocol are converging to make this scenario not only plausible, but also fairly likely.

The executive, however, was adamant. "It simply won't happen that way," he claimed. After all, he reasoned, many construction workers don't use computers on the job. Because they had not been trained on computers, he reasoned, a forecast that showed the use of handheld computer devices on construction sites didn't make sense.

One simple observation jarred the client loose from his assumption: *Even poor kids [in 2000] have PlayStations.* Even the least skilled construction workers of 2015 will have grown up with gaming consoles like PlayStation and Xbox, devices that depend on software, menus, and simple controls. In addition, computers were dropping in price every day, which indicated that the class divide between households that owned computers and those that did not would be reduced by 2015.

This executive could imagine the project manager of 2015 using sophisticated software on and off the job site, but the chief assumption he was harboring was that the construction workers of tomorrow would be the same as they are today, with minimal IT skills. He could not imagine a world where even the poor kids knew how to use simple software systems and, therefore, that by 2015 artisans at all levels could use software-driven devices.

Some assumptions are like that—they are ideas or beliefs we hold, the reasons for which are hidden even to us, that subconsciously color our visions of the future. Assumptions become dangerous, or can at least ruin your day, when they obscure your view of what lies around the corner.

THE ABILITY TO DETECT POTENTIAL THREATS AND OPPORTUNITIES

Threats are a major reason to keep an eye on the future. The future is not always rosy. In well-entrenched, successful organizations, people often forget that bad stuff happens to nice organizations every day. Companies go out of business. Foreign powers act unexpectedly and attack other nations. Stakeholders turn hostile. The value of futures research is that once a potential threat is revealed, you can watch it like a hawk and take countermeasures if and when necessary.

For many businesses, one threatening trend might not be too bad, but if several trends hit at one time, the consequences could be severe—just as they were for the record industry, which had to contend with several new technologies simultaneously. To protect your business from similar disasters, futurism gives you the tools to track potential threats well in advance.

Consider the impact of the convergence of the following trends on farm stores in New England:

- A housing boom, the consolidation of retailing

- The increased power of information technology, which allowed the rise of Big Box stores such as Home Depot and Tractor Supply throughout the country

- The increased use of biotechnology and satellite information systems that increased the economies of scale in large-scale farming

- The migration of farms from New England to the Midwest and California

- The move of Big Box stores into smaller markets to sustain their revenue growth and impress Wall Street

The result for New England farm stores? Farm revenues drop off at the exact moment a giant "category killer" retailer establishes stores in small towns in Vermont, New Hampshire, and Maine. Agway, Inc., a farm store cooperative with a 100-year history in the region, finally sold all its assets to Southern States, another cooperative in a similar strategic fix.

As scary as some of these stories are, don't forget: Although analyzing the future helps us avert facing terrible situations, it also can be used to search for positive developments.

AN UNDERSTANDING OF YOUR ROLE IN HISTORY

One thing most people who use studies of the future have in common is that they are leading large organizations that will probably be around in 15 to 20 years. Coca Cola, the Pentagon, Finland, and other organizations of this size study the future to improve their destinies and to choose the best outcome possible. These groups have another thing in common: They are large, powerful, and are responsible in one way or another for people's lives. They influence people's diets; their health care; war; commerce; communications; and, in some instances, all of human life.

The individuals who run these organizations are often aware of the massive power they have to alter history. They can change the lives of generations of people. Studies of the future allow these leaders to look out and recognize the kind of world they are creating for their children.

Take, for example, the sustainability movement: Industries and governments are coming together and using foresight to make sure that we can continue operating our societies without reducing the ability of our children to meet their needs. Many are troubled to think that our decisions could spell doom and hardship for those who will come after us. By studying the future, we can make positive, proactive decisions to shape our future, not just make individual decisions. There is a tremendous amount to be gained from learning how to choose our future, rather than waiting for it to happen to us.

○ ○ ○

In chapters 2 through 15, I illustrate the forecasting methods used by professional futurists and show you how to use these tools to improve your ability to see what is next and apply its lessons to your business. These tools and illustrations will help you see deeper into the future so you can check your own assumptions, detect threats and opportunities early, and decide what future you want for yourself and your organization.

To master the techniques of professional futurists, we are going to apply them to an exploration of the future of beer. Yes, beer. Beer is a perfect subject for a study of the future. The industry faces subtle but important changes, even though it is indispensable to many people. (At least at barbeques!) What's more, this book wouldn't be as much fun if it took you on a journey through the future of ultrasonic flow meters for sewage-treatment plants. Take it from me . . . I have done that study, too.

By the end of this book, you will understand the trends that will affect the beer industry in the next 10 years. You'll see beer in a broader perspective, explore the hidden trends that will change the industry, and figure out what it means to the brewers of today. Moreover, you will come to discover ways to clearly communicate potential future scenarios, even to people skeptical that the world will be any different.

Likely, you are not in the beer industry, but once you understand the tools, you can study the future to make your next decision. If you are an entrepreneur, you could use your insight to start a new business. If you are in the corporate world, perhaps a new product or service will suddenly seem obvious to you, or you may see a new threat on the horizon. If you are in government, you will see the needs of tomorrow's constituents more clearly. No matter what, once you understand how to see what's coming next, it will change how you see the world and where it's heading. Onward, then, to the future!

CHAPTER TWO

systems thinking

a superhighway to change

What is the future of beer? Quick, off the top of your head, what will the beer of the future be like?

For everybody, in the beer business or not, the question is a bit unfair. Actually, it is impossible to answer without breaking it down, but where should you start? It's a complex question. Nobody, not even futurists, can answer that kind of question without a methodology. In this chapter, I will show you how to broaden your thinking, look beyond your industry, and realize that the future is all around you in an endless number of superconnected systems. The key is to break those systems down into their components, which makes the future more manageable and easier to think about.

This technique will prepare you to follow the future *you* need to keep an eye on. Once you grasp that concept, the future of beer—or the future of any topic—will become more evident to you.

Strategic Thinking Dissected

The future of anything is like an ecosystem. It is made up of a variety of systems and activities. For this reason, the first step any futurist takes in analyzing a business or an industry, whether it's an analysis for Anheuser-Busch or Bob's Corner Store, is to take it apart, system by system, activity by activity, to understand the drivers of change that eventually affect that business. Based on this analysis, the futurist then builds a chart that illustrates the ecosystem of that business or industry. This chart serves as a guide as the futurist engages in the more in-depth examinations of the company's future using trend analysis, forecast generation, and scenarios. Futurists call this stage of the process *systems analysis*. When you have completed this chapter, you will be able to build a systems map of your industry.

To begin, let's have a look at Figure 2–1, which will give you an idea of the various interconnected factors that go into making a single strategic decision.

The decision-maker's world is far more complex than his industry alone. Maybe he's running a small microbrewery. Perhaps he's an exec at a chemical company. Large business or small, he must think about a great deal more than the quality of his product and how many customers have ordered it. New technologies lurk that may let his competitors manufacture substitute products at lower prices. New regulations could change how he does business.

Futures strategy depends on thinking about the world as a system

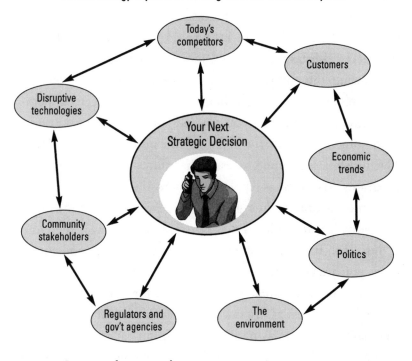

FIGURE 2–1. Ecosystem of a strategic decision.

Economic trends could alter who is able to buy his products. The environment is stressed; he may be concerned about supplies of raw materials or the impact of global warming.

All these changes and events are connected and affect one another. This is as true for business and government as it is for living organisms. Resources are limited, innovation is constant, and there is more symbiosis than out-and-out competition. Understanding the larger system in which your company belongs is crucial to your success.

Thinking of our businesses and ourselves as part of a larger ecosystem is a big step toward understanding where we are going. We are often taught to compare business to war, but rarely, if ever, to biology. Despite the number of times you may have been told or read that "business is war," in reality, wars, soldiers, and battlefields have little to do with it. Battlefields are destructive; businesses to thrive must be creative.

Viewing the future of your business through the lens of "ecosystem analysis" is multilinear, creative, and often cooperative. After all, in business you can find yourself in joint ventures, even sometimes with rivals. Have you noticed that the latest Macintosh has an Intel processor that allows it to run Windows programs? As much as Apple and Microsoft are competing for the same customers, their goal isn't the destruction of the other company; it is to exploit a new opportunity wherever they find it. Just as in nature, sometimes you are competing, and sometimes you are cooperating.

The ecosystem analogy works well for the study of the future because just as organisms interact with each other so do trends. Nothing exists in and of itself, but rather as a web of connections. As the nature of the web changes, so does each part. Therefore, to understand the future of anything, one must begin by considering its ecosystem, whether natural, technological, or social. In a fast-paced, interconnected world, everything affects your market and your mission. Thinking broadly is required not only to be a well-rounded person and an interesting conversationalist at dinner parties, but to make sure your next strategic move is not doomed because you have ignored an essential factor.

Futurists certainly didn't invent this kind of thinking. Not only is it the foundation of modern biology; it is one of the fundamental tenets of Buddhism. I was surprised to see the basic idea behind futurism, brilliantly illustrated by the famed Buddhist monk and author Thich Nhat Hanh in his book *The Heart of Understanding: Commentaries on the Prajnaparamita*

Heart Sutra (which I don't believe is required reading at Wharton). In it, he says:

> . . . you cannot look at paper without seeing the trees that served as raw materials, the soil that nourished the tree, and the rain that made the soil fertile.

This is a beautiful way to describe the first step in the process of looking at the future strategically. When you think about a problem or anything else, no matter how complex, take it apart. If it's a product, find out where its supplies or components came from, who participated in its creation, and where it all began. If you can see all parts of the system, then you have a much better chance of seeing where the next change will come from. This is exactly how futurists look at the world when they lead organizations on their crucial studies of what's on the horizon. Once you get into this habit of thinking, you will see everything through this broader lens and will therefore be better able to uncover the threats—and the opportunities.

Spotting the Trends: The Future of Chocolate

Let's start practicing this kind of strategic thinking by looking at something simple and analyzing the future of its components.

Quick—picture, in your mind's eye, a chocolate bar. Now, what is the future of chocolate bars?

What could be simpler, right? It's chocolate. It contains no computer chips. R&D scientists aren't always improving chocolate. It's just some yummy confection wrapped in foil.

STEEP ANALYSIS

Think again; the future has a lot in store for mundane items like chocolate. Start by thinking about all the different fields that could affect the future of chocolate. To get you started, let's use one of the most basic tools futurists have—the famous STEEP analysis. Well, okay. Maybe it's not famous unless you're a professional futurist. Anyway, it stands for trends in **S**ociety, **T**echnology, **E**conomics, **E**cology, and **P**olitics. This handy mnemonic will help you remember how to frame your thoughts when thinking about the future.

No one on earth is simultaneously an expert in each of these five categories, and the very broadness of each of these terms will make you think about subjects outside your own industry and area of expertise. Here are a few examples of what each of these terms encompasses:

SOCIETY

- Demographics
- Family life
- Public health
- Religion

TECHNOLOGY

- Biotechnology
- Chemistry and materials science
- Information technology
- Manufacturing
- Nanotechnology

ECONOMICS

- Globalization of commerce and labor

○ Poverty and the rich/poor gap

○ Inflation

○ Currency fluctuations

ECOLOGY

○ Global warming

○ Supplies of clean water

○ Topsoil and agricultural systems

○ Air quality

POLITICS

○ International governing bodies

○ Wars and regional conflicts

○ Government regulations and agency oversight

○ Legislative trends, new bills

○ Lawsuits and litigiousness

There are enough topics here to inspire hundreds of doctoral dissertations. If we had to understand all the trends in each of these areas just to understand the future of chocolate, we would have to quit our day jobs. Luckily, not everything on that list applies to the future of chocolate, but if you read down the list and ask yourself what *does* apply, suddenly something that seemed irrelevant a few moments ago rings a bell. The future of chocolate begins to take shape when you begin to examine the trends that will affect it.

DETERMINING RELEVANCE

Let's break it down. Which of the listed topics apply to chocolate? Well, in the *society* column, there is the public health aspect. We've all been reading about the epidemic of childhood obesity, so we should look at trends in health and diet. Insofar as *technology* is concerned, there isn't necessarily a lot that will change the future of chocolate itself, but what about its packaging? There is a great deal happening in materials science that could change how we package food, so maybe the foil wrapper will change.

Economics probably isn't a huge driver, because a chocolate bar is fairly affordable—it's not like buying a car, where you worry about salaries and interest rates. That said, we don't grow cocoa beans in the United States, so we might need to watch currency fluctuations. And what about the price of sugar? When we think about *ecology*, cocoa cultivation can be a big driver behind the destruction of the rain forests. *Politics*, oddly enough, could be an interesting area to consider. With the recent trend in class-action lawsuits, we should probably understand what could happen if consumers decide to hire lawyers and go after candy companies for health-related problems that result from obesity.

Now, let's look at Figure 2–2 to see how we might think about chocolate using the STEEP system.

In this context, this everyday, uncomplicated item, a chocolate bar, is in the middle of a swirling storm of complex, interconnected social and technological change. All of a sudden, something we took for granted is at the forefront of innovation.

RESEARCHING THE TRENDS

What is more important, however, is to understand how these trends interact. It's the interconnection of all these trends at once that causes seemingly chaotic, unexpected change. It is not the trends themselves, but their interaction, that can cause new inventions, such as the MP3, to overwhelm record companies.

For now, we want to practice thinking about things as systems; later, you will develop the ability to understand the implications

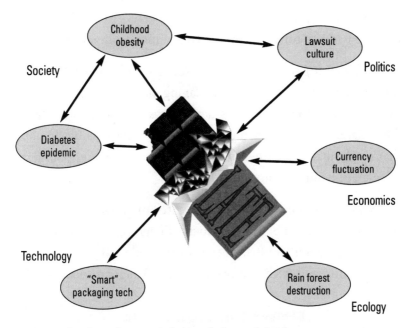

FIGURE 2–2. Ecosystem of a strategic decision: the future of chocolate.

of all these interactions—that is, to see a complex system and figure out what it means.

Let's look at the chocolate system to see what the trends that could be researched are and see how their interactions could affect the candy industry. We'll start with some basic trend research I've done (see Figure 2–3).

Thinking about materials science, continued destruction of the rain forests, recent trends in diabetes, the price of cocoa and sugar, currency fluctuations, and an increase in class-action lawsuits in a variety of industries was crucial to seeing beyond the familiar and getting at what may affect the future of chocolate. Why?

"Evil Candy Companies." Child obesity is reaching epic proportions, and there are so many kids getting adult-onset diabetes that they had to change the name to "type II diabetes."

The public may come to blame the marketers of candy just as they now blame tobacco and pharmaceutical companies.

Class-Action Lawsuits. Now that states have successfully pursued tobacco companies for damaging public health, lawyers may be willing to take on class-action lawsuits and go after "Big Chocolate."[1] After all, somebody has to be responsible for all that costly diabetes care, especially because more and younger people are being diagnosed with it.

"Smart Packaging." More sophisticated materials and biosensors will change the way products, including chocolate, are wrapped. The foil wrapper of tomorrow could tell you whether anyone tampered with the product. RFID tags, if made small

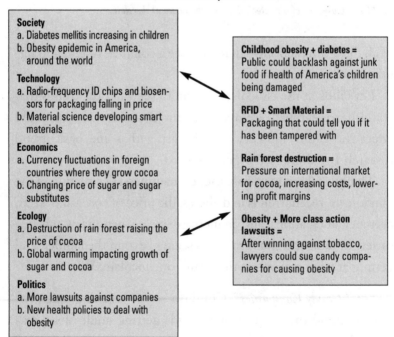

Interconnected STEEP Analysis on Chocolate

Society
a. Diabetes mellitis increasing in children
b. Obesity epidemic in America, around the world

Technology
a. Radio-frequency ID chips and biosensors for packaging falling in price
b. Material science developing smart materials

Economics
a. Currency fluctuations in foreign countries where they grow cocoa
b. Changing price of sugar and sugar substitutes

Ecology
a. Destruction of rain forest raising the price of cocoa
b. Global warming impacting growth of sugar and cocoa

Politics
a. More lawsuits against companies
b. New health policies to deal with obesity

Childhood obesity + diabetes =
Public could backlash against junk food if health of America's children being damaged

RFID + Smart Material =
Packaging that could tell you if it has been tampered with

Rain forest destruction =
Pressure on international market for cocoa, increasing costs, lowering profit margins

Obesity + More class action lawsuits =
After winning against tobacco, lawyers could sue candy companies for causing obesity

FIGURE 2–3. Trend research: the candy industry.

enough, could tell retailers if someone steals or diverts a product from its destination.

Threats to the Rain Forest. Because cocoa cultivation endangers the rain forest, will companies have to substitute some other ingredient for it?

Viewing everything we do as part of a larger system introduces us to a world that is constantly evolving, even when we think that the subject of our study is relatively straightforward—like chocolate bars. This quick look at the future of the chocolate business demonstrates that each aspect of the system—from the rain forest to public health—is on the move. We live in exciting times, because so many things—even the chocolate industry—are evolving.

To practice thinking like a futurist, first get rid of the notion that some things don't change. Maybe you think that, sure, computers are changing, but what I do is really "old school," traditional, and not much is really happening. Many people miss major changes and great opportunities by thinking that change is for other people and other industries. As we've seen, if change can happen to chocolate, it can happen to you.

Diagramming the System: The Future of Water

We've explored the STEEP system to get you thinking more broadly about the future. The point of systems thinking is not to *discover* the future; it is to provide a starting point for the coming work. In a real futures study, like the one we will do for beer, we start by creating a systems diagram that will tell us which trends we really need to study.

To illustrate how this is done, I will apply the techniques to a futures study for a global corporation. Remember that the changes in global trends are just as important for smaller businesses as they are for large companies. Whether your revenue is $100,000 a year or many billions, a fundamental change in the future can still mean a threat or an opportunity. Let's dive into a real-world project and put together a full, formal systems diagram on the future of water. Thinking broadly and diagramming the system is always the first step in a rigorous futures study, because this view informs everything that you study later.

Since the time of the Roman aqueducts, the water business hasn't changed much, but purification techniques and filter technologies are always improving, courtesy of materials science. From a consumer's perspective, water is not a fast-paced industry, but in 2002, a client came to me concerned about the future of water. As one of the largest infrastructure-engineering firms in the world, this client builds large water systems for municipalities, bringing clean potable water cheaply to the public.

The reason for this client's sudden interest in the future was that some executives at the company were becoming spooked because for the first time in their lives the very business of water was changing in a fundamental way. More and more people were buying branded bottled water: Dasani, Poland Spring, Aquafina, and others. Soft-drink suppliers were selling ever more water at prices hundreds of times the price at the tap. Clearly, a basic shift in the water business was under way.

To the executives in the engineering firm, each an expert on water purity, this trend bordered on ludicrous. After all, many of these fancy $0.99 per bottle brands are little more than filtered tap water bottled and chilled. Still, the trend was jarring, and the leaders of this company asked an important question: "Do we know as much about the future as we should?" Their basic question was, "What is the future of water?"

Here's where systems analysis comes in handy. Because the question is so complex, the first step is to map what went into the water "system" before we start any trend research. It is a time to ask basic questions about water. When I start a study like this, I ask, "What does water do all day?" Instead of looking only at the business of water, we looked at water from all sides:

○ Where does water come from?

○ What purpose does water serve?

○ Who works with water?

○ What can go wrong?

The executives were worried about the radical shift toward bottled water, causing them to ask:

○ Did consumers no longer trust them?

○ Was there a perception in consumers' minds of an environmental danger from municipal water systems that made tap water seem dangerous?

○ Is that why people were starting to pay more for filtered tap water in a plastic bottle?

Our systems analysis would search broadly for the answers to these questions. To begin, we developed a diagram for water, stepping through all the ways to analyze H_2O.

STEP 1: TELL THE STORY AND DIAGRAM IT
To communicate the story of the future graphically, flow charts work well (see Figure 2–4).

Think of systems analysis as just another story, with actors, a plot, and some kind of transformation. This is a rare opportunity: You get to explore the story of water (or chocolate or semiconductors), and because, in all probability, nobody is likely working on the same topic, you have a fascinating and original task.

To begin any study, ask yourself a basic question; in this case, "Where does water come from?" Then track it from there.

Well, water comes from rain, moisture, streams, oceans, the atmosphere, etc. Then, it goes into the groundwater system, then drains, and then the municipal water system. From rain to drain, we were interested in everything that water might go through—and what might change. The fact that water travels through pipes is a guide to what to think about next. The water table is the upper limit of groundwater. The water needs to be pumped out of the earth through a well or sent through a municipal water system. Many engineers and a great deal of local infrastructure—including (among other things) testing, filtering, pumps, and pipes—are required to get this water to a municipal water system. Only then does the water find its end user, be it for manufacturing or other

Diagram the activity—
Get it on paper so you can see it all in one spot

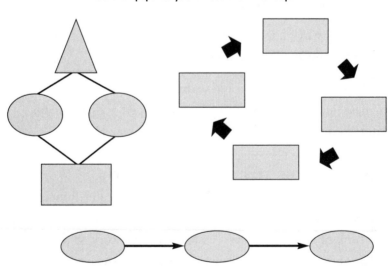

FIGURE 2–4. Systems analysis: basic diagram format.

The Water System

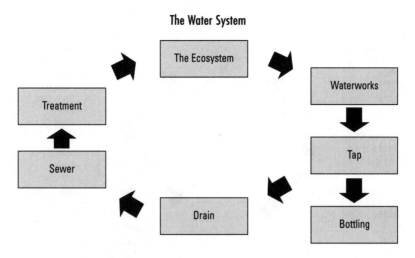

FIGURE 2–5. Telling the story: the water system.

industrial uses, watering crops, or satisfying a thirsty six-year-old who wants some Kool-Aid.

Because this is all a cycle, the water finds its way back to the water table, either through sewage treatment or straight into streams and lakes. For every stop in the cycle, every part of the system, new facets of the overall business ecosystem become evident.

We can now map it out. Add boxes for each part of the system. Notice that in Figure 2–5, I map the ecosystem from which the water comes, the waterworks that will transport it to the home, the tap, then back down the drain. Starting the diagram this way gives you a frame on which to hang all you know about the future—which is likely more than you initially imagined.

STEP 2: IDENTIFY THE PLAYERS

Think of everybody who might be involved. Who touches your industry or activity today? Employees? Consumers? Leaders? Competitors? Supporters? Skeptics?

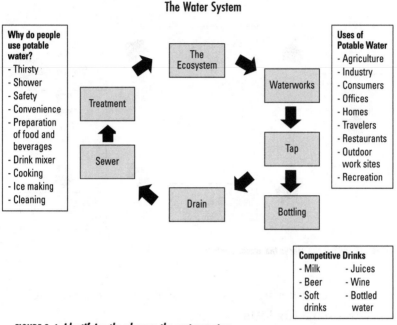

FIGURE 2–6. Identifying the players: the water system.

What are they up to? How are they changing? What are their problems? What will make them change in the future? If *your job* still exists in 2020, what will it be like? How will the person who holds that job think? What will be the same? What might be radically different? Figure 2–6 captures this thought process.

STEP 3: DETERMINE THE TRENDS AND FORCES AFFECTING THE SYSTEM

We have not begun the actual trend research yet. However, to remind ourselves of our goal, we sketched potential trends and put them into the diagram. To determine which trends we hoped to explore, we asked questions such as:

○ What are the major technologies used in the water business?

○ Are they advancing?

○ Is anything radically new and different on the horizon?

○ Will these new technologies require different people with different skills to work in this activity?

○ Will the consumers of water be different? Will their expectations change?

○ What *wild-card* events might also affect the system? Is terrorism a factor?

Figure 2–7 is our graphic illustrating the water system. No question, this is extremely complex, but the client wanted details. Not every chart has to contain this level of detail. Note

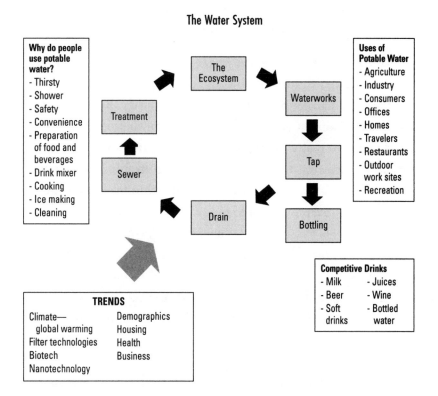

FIGURE 2–7. Determining trends and forces: the water system.

also that the trends don't follow STEEP exactly. It's intended as a good point of departure to guide you to the trends that are most applicable to your subject.

The Value of Systems Thinking

Remember, this is only step one of a much larger process, and diagramming is only a launching point. This systems analysis was the beginning of an ongoing project that helped an engineering firm understand the shifting marketplace of the water industry. This is the tool that leads to trend analysis and forecasting—techniques we will discuss in chapters 3 and 4.

The systems diagram helps identify otherwise hidden trends in the future of water. After weeks of thorough trend research, this initial systems map led us to the following conclusions:

Water is becoming "health food." Many consumers associate water with health for the obvious reasons as well as because of very careful marketing by the beverage industry. Because water is packaged almost as a "health tonic," it turned out that water engineers are really in the health business, and water providers are in fact experts in what makes water healthful or dangerous. This knowledge was a way for the company to find a new niche for itself; for example, "come to our firm when you want to use municipal water as another vehicle for public health."

Also, we pointed out that "nutraceuticals," a combination of food plus nutrients and vitamins designed to encourage good health, were on the rise. It is interesting to note that some years after our study, there was a proliferation of water beverages fortified with vitamins B6 and B12, ginseng, minerals, and other additives to promote health.

As a result of our study, the engineering firm realized that, in the future, consumers might want to mix their own water beverages based on their specific health regimens, and therefore that the company might consider providing equipment that would let customers dial in the mix of minerals, fluoride, vitamins, or any other nutritional supplement to their water. A one-size-fits-one approach to custom manufacturing (or "mass customization") is on the rise in other industries; the water business may follow this paradigm.

It's a big leap for city water systems who think of themselves as infrastructure engineers, not consumer products companies!

Water systems need to be sustainable, restoring natural systems. Water engineers are becoming caretakers of our natural systems as the swelling population taxes water tables. Bottled water or not, it was clear that in the future there would be a strong need for those who could bring and keep a water ecosystem in balance. In the western United States where farms and cities steal water from faraway water tables without replacing it, cities would want to be sure their water comes from a safe place and that the supply would continue into the future.

The water infrastructure requires increasing security. In a world menaced by global terror, terrorism would increase as a risk (either real or perceived) and the need for water security would provide opportunities for the engineering firm to expand into new businesses. Sadly, this is going to be a growth industry.

World population is growing and the size of cities in developing economies is exploding. The biggest market for fresh water is the 50 percent of the world's population without daily access to any. Population growth is very high in countries like Nigeria, Bangladesh, and China. Combine this with rapid urbanization worldwide, and you have cities in developing economies that will need infrastructure to meet the need for water as they swell with people from the countryside. If the engineering firm wasn't already taking a global view of its business, now would have been a good time to start.

Systems Thinking: The Future of Beer

We warmed up with water and its uses, using as our first example a systems map from an actual project. Now we have serious work to do in analyzing the future of beer. Its destiny is in our hands! Like water, beer is a potable liquid that many people count on for health (and entertainment); therefore, the diagrams will look surprisingly similar.

To get this chart started, imagine the beer cycle and all the different factors that go into making beer; the flows (literal and figurative) all over the world; and the consequences, healthy and otherwise, of beer consumption. Here are all the activities I imagined; you may have imagined others:

- Agriculture
  - Hops, wheat, barley
  - Water
- Brewing
- Packaging
- Shipping
- Distribution and retailing
- Consumers
- Waste and recycling
- Government regulation
- Social impact
- New technologies
- Competing beverages

From this, let's make a flow chart to see what happens to beer (Figure 2–8).

FIGURE 2–8. Flow chart: the beer system.

CONSTRUCTING A FLOW CHART: THE STORY OF BEER

To create a convincing beer system, the diagram should tell the story of beer at a glance. So let us recap the story. If you are American, you have likely heard the story of beer a million times from Budweiser commercials during football games. Brewers lovingly seek out fresh hops and barley and use only the freshest mountain stream water to brew beer. Thus, we start with agriculture as the source of raw materials needed for the brewing process. We also know that once the beer is aged and ready for consumption, it is packaged in kegs, bottles, or cans to be shipped out to distribution centers all over the world, all under the watch of strict regulation. The beer then arrives at retail outlets, such as package stores, grocery stores, bars, or restaurants. Finally, the beer reaches the consumer, who discards the packaging.

Next, I would add some of the trends in STEEP that could be important to the beer business. Will biotechnology change the growing of grains or fermenting of alcohol? Health trends in obesity and alcoholism could be important. Packaging technology is often a big deal. Will it change how beer is shipped and retailed? Figure 2–9 shows the new chart.

That's enough for now. At this stage, our diagram need not explain every facet of beer to provide us with a systems map that will guide us through the real work—collecting and interpreting trends and forecasts so we can communicate the future to others or make decisions for our own business.

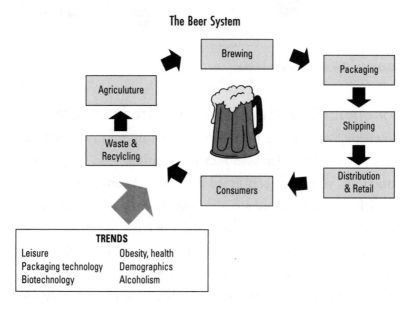

FIGURE 2–9. Flow chart: impact of trends on the beer system.

By the Way, Systems Thinking Is Fun

If you are like many people today, this kind of broad thinking is a real departure. One of the reasons that systems thinking is so effective in helping executives think more clearly about the future is . . . it's fun! For those who have climbed the ranks of their respective industries, executives in charge of strategy have had to master an incredible array of detailed information about a narrow sliver of a business, whether marketing for pharmaceuticals or evaluating technologies for satellite imagery. Successful leaders who use futures research love this kind of broader thinking because they can break away and get creative. Entrepreneurs and small-business owners enjoy keeping on top of future trends because they can react the fastest to capitalize on the future. They don't have the disadvantage of large, unwieldy bureaucracy. For large and small, thinking broad is what keeps business interesting.

CHECKLIST: Systems Thinking

- ✔ Look broad. Remember STEEP—society, technology, economics, ecology, and politics.

- ✔ Draw it out. Make a systems map to show how things interconnect.

- ✔ Print it out—show your colleagues the systems map to broaden their thinking.

WHAT YOU CAN DO TODAY

1. Put up a systems diagram of your company or industry. Sit down, alone, or with a few colleagues, and brainstorm everything surrounding your industry. Include trends and customers. Get it on one piece of paper.

2. Hang the systems map on your desk for you to see, or on your door for your colleagues to see. This makes sure you constantly know which part of the horizon you should be looking at.

3. Want an even bigger reminder? Print out copies and distribute to everyone in your company. As much as lots of companies talk about "thinking about the future," very rarely is that perspective spread throughout, from top to bottom. You can make the future part of everything you do by making it a group effort.

analyzing trends

real change vs. media hype

Now that you have determined all the different factors that will change the future of the beer industry, notably agriculture, brewing, packaging, and consumption, you are probably chomping at the bit to seek out the hardcore trend data, hungry for that hidden information that will reveal the future. (Am I the only one who gets so excited by this stuff?)

Regardless, before I throw you into the deep ocean of information, you need to understand the tricky nature of the elusive *future trend.*

If It's a Big Deal in the Media, It Must Be Important

The summer before the nation was transfixed by the events of September 11, the media was abuzz with a different sort of threat—this time to America's children. No, not violent video games or an epidemic of ADHD—this was a threat more silent and more vicious. The summer of 2001 was the Summer of the Shark. Do you remember the headlines? The media was obsessed. Experts commented endlessly on shark behavior. Swimmers were warned. Talking heads fretted. The news was full of detailed analyses of every aspect of sharks and their appetite for humans. There was just one teensy-weensy point the media forgot to mention. Shark attacks were actually lower than average in 2001.

According to the ichthyology department of the Florida Museum of Natural History:

> The prevailing perception was that 2001 was a banner year for shark attacks. The year 2002 attack totals, both nationally and internationally, were lower than those in 2001 and 2000, continuing a three-year trend of decline in shark-human interactions and underscoring the scientific view that the events of mid-2001 were largely overstated. More importantly, the number of serious attacks in 2001 and 2002, as measured by fatality rate, was about one-third of that over the last decade.[1]

This story is a perfect illustration of the importance of gathering expert trend data when you are conducting any futures study in order to challenge your assumptions. Most of our assumptions, particularly the least accurate, are born from casual impressions we get from the media. To get a clear view of the future, you need to know how to get accurate data about trends from reliable sources.

How to Determine When a Trend Is Really a Trend

The official definition of a trend is quite broad: *any change that happens over time.* Right now, the sun is gradually dying and in several billion years may cease to sustain life on Earth. That's a trend, though one so slow you'll probably not need to warn anybody about it at the next board meeting.

Another trend is that health care costs in America have been outpacing wage growth by several percentage points each year for the last eight years, and the growth shows no sign of abating—*that's* one trend that is causing some heart palpitations.

You know from our discussion about thinking systematically that a tremendous amount is changing in the world, often even in areas we think are stable. As a result, 50 percent of the time involved in futures analysis is spent picking apart trends. You will be looking at articles, reports, books, and anywhere else you can get good information. Once you learn what is really changing, you can see the future with greater clarity.

The world is on the move. Your goal is to figure out exactly how in order to determine how it will affect your business, what you can do to take advantage of the opportunities change might offer, and how you can protect yourself against potential threats. Here are the three steps to successful trend analysis.

STEP 1: DEVELOP YOUR SYSTEMS MAP

When you explore the future of anything, from national parks to air travel and beer, you could become overwhelmed trying to think of everything changing all at once. The systems map you constructed to kick off your study will keep you focused.

Remember that when we looked at the future of potable water we didn't just dive into the trends. Instead, we started our research by first examining what things affected the water system, including health, ecological sustainability, and population trends. In this fashion, you discover where you need to go to get the real data.

STEP 2: VISUALIZE TRENDS

When you begin looking at trends, instead of picking up a 200-page report, be curious. Ask questions related to your project, whatever they might be. For beer, for example, I'm wondering:

○ Who drinks beer these days? Is that changing?

○ Are brewers making beer any differently?

○ Alcoholism is a serious health problem. Is that changing these days? Do people expect beer companies to take greater responsibility?

○ Recycling aluminum cans and glass bottles was important a few years ago. Is that changing?

○ China and India are always on the radar these days when it comes to the future. How might those two billion people change the beer industry?

○ Are new technologies such as biotechnology or nanotechnology likely to change beer?

The questions you might ask are limited only by your imagination and the direction you decide to take. Once you have defined your questions, it's time to find the answers by investigating the best possible sources of information.

STEP 3: LOCATE SOURCES

In studies of the future, getting data is easy, but getting accurate, relevant data collected in a rigorous manner and reported with minimal bias is not easy. You cannot just hop on the Internet and find page after page of well-researched, unbiased data about the future of your topic. It's not *quite* that simple. You will have to do a little digging to find the best information for your study, but don't worry, with a little effort, you'll have more than enough data to show you what is changing. Here are some approaches to try.

BEGIN WITH WHAT'S HAPPENING TODAY. Look at the systems map we created for beer. From it we know that we are going to be looking for future trends in unexpected places: packaging, information technology, geriatrics, all kinds of topics. You can't possibly be an expert in all of these fields. If you try to start by accumulating future data on all of these topics, you'll probably pull a muscle. Do yourself a favor and start reading about *today* just to warm up—it will point the way to all the future trends.

Fortunately, there are magazines devoted to nearly every activity on earth, five magazines for every profession out there, and thousands of websites on anything you can imagine. Are you looking at your systems map and concerned that nobody is writing about the topic? Think again. There are *Hispanic Engineer*; *Scientific Computing & Instrumentation*; *Bass Player*; *New England Booming* (for Baby Boomers in New England, you know); *Knitting*; and my favorite example, *Walking*. That's right, there's a magazine called *Walking*, which you've probably seen at the bookstore a million times but never opened. Clearly, there are magazines for every activity in which humans engage, so it is likely that you will find a trade or consumer magazine that will give you a place to start. Read these magazines to get a sense of the concerns of the people involved in the field.

Watch the ads. Read the "From the Editor" sections to see what they are saying to their peers. Read the articles, jargon and all. Not only will you expand your perspective by seeing how different people view the same topic, but you will begin to make connections among the industries as well.

Imagine the things you will learn as you expand your reading in a variety of fields. For example:

○ You begin reading about sustainability and discover that the experts are concerned about the metrics used to measure sustainable systems, or that they are worried that nobody has found a good way to compensate companies trying to be ecologically and socially sustainable.

○ You read a magazine about retirement and instantly get a sense that the real estate market for retirees is booming. The most desirable places offer peace and quiet, activities, and low taxes, which are attractive to people on fixed incomes. You also realize that those places are in ever-shorter supply.

○ As you quickly flip through *Bass Player* magazine, you find that the bass community is concerned that the increased use of computer software is making music too automated.

Whatever the topic, a quick read through the monthly or quarterly periodicals will get you thinking about the changes that are occurring all around you. In addition, at least once a year, most industrial magazines publish an issue dedicated to future trends. These issues are often popular with the mainstream media. If something significant is changing, it becomes newsworthy. If it makes it into the news, you can read about it and capture it for your analysis.

With all this newspaper and magazine reading I am recommending, don't think that I'm neglecting the Internet. Doing research on the Internet is, as anyone who has tried knows, like trying to take a sip from a fire hose going full blast, but it's great, during this warm-up period, for getting a sense of what's going on today.

To return to our analysis of the future of beer, for example, you can get 100 quick data points just by Googling the words "future beer trends." In under a second, you can begin sampling opinions at www.allaboutbeer.com, in *Packaging News*, and in newspaper articles about gourmet beer and what proponents of the low-carb lifestyle think about beer. During this initial round of trend research, collection should be freeflowing. Don't worry if it leads to more questions than answers. Ask yourself:

- What trends are most important to the industry?

- Is there a common topic that keeps coming up in the different sources?

- What names or key institutions keep popping up?

- Who are the thought leaders in the field?

Next, it's time for the heavy research. Look for reliable sources. Even though I have recommended that you spend your initial time researching popular sources of information, I have to warn you: *Magazines are not going to cut it 99 percent of the time. Two mentions in* Newsweek *do not a trend make.* Sure, the popular media will give you a good overview and help get you started, but at this point your view of the future is shallow. It's time to get serious, to go where the experts go to stay abreast of the cutting edge in their own fields.

Below are the two most reliable sources available to you, presented in order of their reliability and credibility.

PEER-REVIEWED AND SCHOLARLY JOURNALS. Peer-reviewed journals represent the cutting edge of any industry. The *Journal of Clinical Pharmacology* may be difficult to read if you aren't a pharmacist, but the information it contains is certain to be on the leading edge of pharmacology. More important, experts police peer-reviewed journals so they don't contain unsubstantiated claims, and you can be certain that the information is highly reliable because in the sciences and other serious disciplines, falsifying data in front of your peers is career suicide if it is discovered.

There are drawbacks, certainly. Don't expect broad thinking in these magazines. It is not what the experts writing for them do! Thus, the data you find in these journals is likely to be reliable about a specific subject but won't reveal much about "the future" in its larger sense. This is because the research tends to focus on narrow slices of any particular field. You will get details, not perspective.

Examples of peer-reviewed journals you might use in your futures research include:

- *Journal of the American Medical Association*
- *American Bar Association Journal*
- *Journal of Sustainable Agriculture*
- *Nanotechnology*

OFFICIAL REPORTS. Universities, government agencies, nongovernmental organizations (NGOs), and other large groups often release, at no charge to the public, reports of their research activities. These are useful to the futurist because the objective of the groups sponsoring these studies usually is to influence decision makers, and they often have the resources to do the job correctly.

Let's say you are interested in the future of family life around the world. Your company sells products directed toward consumers, and to understand where the family is going is of vital importance. The U.S. Census reports on demographic trends and often includes related economic data. A report from the Census can tell you what is happening to family finances in America in a way that few private organizations ever could. In other countries, like Brazil, NGOs might study family trends to understand the gap between the rich and the poor and its effect on the family unit. Those studies might be detailed and based on data collected by the United Nations, which is another organization with significant resources. Scholars and researchers at universities are no doubt studying a variety of aspects of family life, for example, the effects of two parents working outside of the home.

Reports coming from these agencies will be reliable for the most part, but you must be aware of potential biases of the researchers. Some reports, such as the U.S. Census, are entirely data driven and interpretations are based on statistical analysis. Also, many government agencies inoculate themselves from potential criticism by preparing detailed reports documenting the facts behind their conclusions.

Remember that some organizations, especially activist groups, have no obligation to rigorous, unbiased data. They are working to convince you to adopt their view of the world and thus aren't necessarily impartial. This is not to suggest that all activists traffic in biased information, but you need to read with a critical eye.

I discovered this while working on a project on the future of sustainable agriculture. Before doing any research whatsoever, I assumed that topsoil erosion and groundwater pollution were increasing faster than ever. After all, I had heard about pollution caused by large-scale factory farming and the terrible loss of topsoil for years. It seemed reasonable that after all these years without any good news, it was probably as bad as ever.

Yet, once I concluded the initial phase of my research, it appeared that there had been many initiatives in the previous 30 years to preserve topsoil and clean water. I began to wonder if the topsoil was still eroding. And, if it was, was there more or less erosion than 30 years prior? In short, what is the trend? Are topsoil loss and groundwater pollution getting better or worse?

Many of the environmental-activist organizations I researched consistently criticized large-scale farming. Their reports included statistics about the loss of millions of cubic feet of topsoil and the many millions of gallons of chemicals washed into the water system. It sounded like the situation was bad, yet the data were not particularly well sourced. It wasn't clear which study produced these dire assessments. What set off alarms for me was that *nowhere did these reports say if the situation was better or worse*. In addition, there were no forecasts about the future, whether the problem would one day drop off the radar, or if things would one day reach a crisis point. All I heard about was that factory farming was "bad."

The Department of Agriculture weighed in with its data on the environment, saying that the situation needed improvement but was getting steadily better. Topsoil loss still appeared to be an issue, but conservation initiatives were gradually reducing the impact of farming, even while improving crop yields.

I suspect that activists were afraid of calling a situation in need of improvement "getting better," concerned that people might stop worrying about the problem. This type of bias or spin is common, and you need to be on the alert for it in the reports you read. In fact, bias is a major reason to get multiple kinds of trend data before drawing conclusions. Even if activist groups don't publish false information, they might leave out key data, which might lead you in another direction. If you read particularly alarming data, for example, a trend that says, "We're losing 10 percent of all bird species each year," you should make sure you verify it with other sources.

In a world that moves as fast as ours does, sensational problems sometimes arise, but if it's really an issue, more than one expert will be covering it. If, for some reason, there is only one expert and that expert's objectivity is questionable, take the data, note the source, and move on. You might not want to base conclusions about the future on one source, but it's equally important not to throw out unorthodox viewpoints!

What to Do When There Is Not Enough Data

It can be difficult to get many kinds of trend data. The supply of unbiased researchers roaming about collecting and analyzing data for the common good on an infinite number of topics is limited. I remember a project I was involved in concerning the future of food trends around the world. My assignment was to find future food trends in the United States and Canada. There generally is quite a bit going on in the U.S. The rate of obesity in the U.S. is well known; the billions of dollars spent on diet foods prove it. Americans are not purists about new kinds of food, as Europeans tend to be, so there are many engineered foods, such as sugar-free sweeteners and "functional foods" infused with vitamins, minerals, and herbs.

But researching Canadian food trends was more difficult. Not many people are writing about Canadian food trends, although, culturally, Canada is similar to the United States in terms of consumption trends. Obesity and diabetes rates are similar to those in the U.S. Diet food consumption is similar to that in the U.S.

So, what was I going to say about Canadian food trends? After evaluating Canadian medical journals and trade magazines, I concluded that because Canadian food trends were so similar to those of their southern neighbor, there hadn't been much published trend analysis. It is a good example of making conclusions based on less than an optimum amount of data.

Do your best, and when you think you have found the best available data, move on.

Deciphering Trends: What Part of the Curve Are We On?

Now it is time to figure out the *kinds* of trends you have unearthed.

One of my favorite cartoons is *Dilbert,* by Scott Adams. One day, as punishment, Dilbert is forced to eat with two economists and somehow survive their conversation. One begins, "The economy is getting better." The other replies, "No it isn't." It was a painfully dull lunch, but a good example of how many people look at the same set of data and come to different conclusions.

Data is often easy to find, but telling what *kind* of trend you are observing can be tricky. When you begin to look at trends, you start at a moment in history. The past is behind you and the future is open in front of you. I usually think in terms of 10 to 100 years in the past and 5 to 20 years into the future. The goal of trend research is to see where we have been and where we are headed. In this way, trends are stories about "what's happening out there."

Be careful. Remember trends aren't forecasts. They are just graphical representations of the data thus far collected. From there, we can extrapolate to see the future. In Chapter 4, we'll look at why it's best to let the experts handle the view forward.

Several kinds of trend curves can help us visualize where the data might be leading.

LINEAR TRENDS

At first blush, linear trends are the easiest to understand—something is changing at a steady rate. Figure 3–1 shows three linear trends. The one going up represents health care costs, which are going up around 9 percent a year in the United States. When will it stop? We know water tables are falling in the Middle East and the western United States. They are represented by the line going down. How low can they go? The horizontal line represents America's birth rate, which is flat at approximately two babies per woman.

The real question to ask when thinking about the future is, When might a trend change? For example, what will make the cost of health care stop increasing indefinitely? When are we going to change our water-use patterns? Alternatively, will some ecosystems completely run out of fresh water?

S CURVE

When you see an S-curve trend with rapid growth, the questions you should be asking are, Can this continue forever? Is there

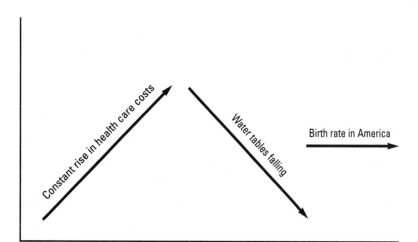

FIGURE 3–1. Linear trends: up, down, flat.

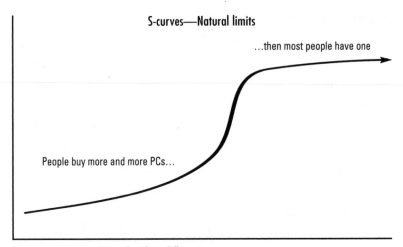

FIGURE 3–2. S curve: rising sharply and flattening out.

some natural limit to this growth? For example, consider the number of home computers: A drop in price opens up the market to millions more people, but eventually you run out of homes without PCs. That creates a sudden increase followed by a plateau, as shown in Figure 3–2.

PARABOLIC CURVE

Parabolic curves indicate that we are on the cusp of a new era. That kind of trend starts small and then explodes exponentially. The growth in the number of users of the Internet is a good example of a parabolic curve (see Figure 3–3).

We were at the "elbow" of that curve in about 1992. It was a golden age for the geeks of the world. The number of Internet users had been relatively flat since the 1970s. Only government scientists and researchers at a few universities connected to the Advanced Research Projects Administration Network used this network, which connected computers for instant digital communication. In the early 1990s, it expanded to include more universities.

By 1994, America Online was expanding rapidly. The World Wide Web made its debut in 1995. The Internet blossomed, and it seemed everybody was online. The growth, as represented in the trend line, was exponential.

When you see this kind of trend, ask yourself how far up the curve we are. Is it likely to flatten out anytime soon? This is still a good question to ask about Internet use. How many of the remaining inhabitants on Earth will be going online? When will this exponential growth slow down?

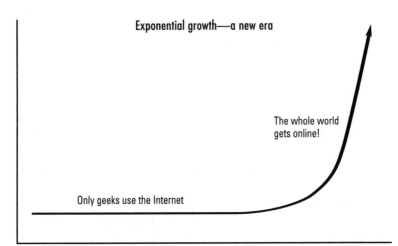

FIGURE 3–3. Parabolic curve: exponential growth.

REVERSE PARABOLA

This is the opposite of the exponential parabolic curve, and a disruptive event that signals big changes usually causes it. For example, vendors once went around cities and towns selling ice to cool iceboxes. As soon as cheap electricity and appliances became available, the ice vendors quickly disappeared. As pictured in Figure 3–4, this is an example of an exponential decline.

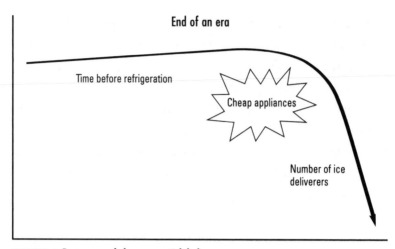

FIGURE 3–4. Reverse parabola: exponential decline.

○ ○ ○

When you look at trends, it is important to think of the different directions that a trend may be going. If you see something changing, ask yourself if the trend is linear, a curve, or a parabola. Then imagine the impact the trend could have on your future. Will it continue to be a factor? Might it flatten out soon and no longer be a problem? Are you on the cusp of a new era?

Case Study: Trends Affecting the Future of Beer!

In Chapter 2, we explored a systems map for beer. Now we can use it to guide our trend analysis. Our goal is to seek trends that tell us what in the beer system is changing that will affect its future. Figure 3–5 shows the systems map of beer.

SOURCES OF INFORMATION

Some topics require a great deal of scholarly research in many heavy academic journals to give you a sense of the future. Fortunately, beer is not one of those topics. On the other hand, you're not going to get a real view of the future of biotechnology without reading some very complex scientific ideas. Although beer is central to many people's lives, not to mention being a multibillion-dollar business, a Ph.D. isn't required to comprehend trends in the industry. It is a very insular, family-run kind of business, even when the companies are public. There are traditions that go back hundreds of years, and brewing often can be traced back several generations. Just ask August Busch IV, current CEO of Anheuser-Busch. As a result, there are only so many people talking and writing about beer as a business, and frequently their remarks are full of inside jokes. One thing you get a definite sense of is a love of the craft and its history. From growing hops to designing new cans and bottles, brewing industry people love beer.

What follows is a list of beer information sources. I found them just as you would. I poked around Google and tried to read everything the beer professionals might read.

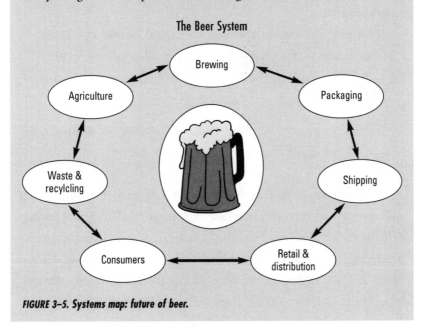

FIGURE 3–5. Systems map: future of beer.

○ *Modern Brewery* magazine

○ Allaboutbeer.com

○ Harvard analysis of trends in the brewing industry

○ Associated Press and various periodicals

○ Reports from the provincial government of Alberta, Canada

○ Official meeting minutes from the European Brewers Convention

ANALYZING THE TRENDS

Although there are few universities doing cutting-edge research on beer technology, our study of beer benefits from lots of casual sources and experts writing about trends to give us a clear view of beer's future. Here are the trends my research revealed as well as my analysis of what they could mean for the beer industry:

CONSUMPTION

○ Overall per capita consumption of alcoholic beverages increased in the United States, from 24.7 gallons in 1995 to 25.2 gallons in 2002—but beer did not take part in this increase.[2]

○ In America, brewers are battling for share-of-stomach, while wine and spirits are increasing strongly.[3]

This is a key trend. Judging by the editorials in some of its industry periodicals, the beer industry is worried that it is losing relevance, but this trend seals it. Americans are drinking as many alcoholic beverages as before, but they are swinging away from beer, that all-American beverage. If this trend increases over the next 10 to 15 years, then "Beer 2020" could look very different when we come around to writing scenarios! Here is some more trend information:

- ○ "Malternative" beverages such as Smirnoff Ice exploded onto the market in 2001 and 2002, selling 23 million cases before falling by eight million cases in 2003 and slumping even further in recent years.[4]

- ○ Although in 2004 "fresh cohorts of 21-year-olds enter the drinking population," many new drinkers are choosing beverages other than beer. Beer consumption among young people, once the core demographic for beer, is dropping precipitously—market preference for beer among this group dropped from 71 percent in 1992 to 48 percent in 2005.[5] Spirits consumption increased 3.1 percent in 2004, while wine jumped 2.7 percent. The 21–34 year-old demographic is being increasingly wooed to premium vodkas and pinot noir by aggressive ad campaigns brewers have been unable to match.[6]

It's hard to imagine anybody marketing more aggressively than beer companies do, but apparently they are losing ground. Despite their advertising, the preference for beer is falling sharply. The numbers tell the story. The total volume of wine and spirits sales has been increasing steadily while sales of beer are stagnant. Young people are an important part of the demographic for beer, and if the younger generations are going for sweeter, more refined beverages such as vodka and wine, there is trouble on the horizon.

Sweet "Malternatives," such as Smirnoff Ice, were strong a few years ago but are losing market share. Beer sales seem to be losing ground to other beverages, and it looks like the winners will be classic spirits such as vodka, rum, and wine. But consider this trend:

○ Craft beer volume is climbing steadily, growing 7 percent in 2004 alone.[7]

This trend demonstrates that not that all beer sales are slumping. Flavorful microbrews are growing rapidly. Maybe the big beer companies like Budweiser, Miller, and Coors will acquire more microbreweries or develop new recipes. I need more trend data to see how this will come out. What about this?

○ Preference for wine is increasing sharply among all demographics. In 1992, only 27 percent of the population favored wine, whereas 47 percent preferred beer. Today, wine and beer are preferred equally.[8]

Without the data, you might not have believed this trend. Not long ago, nobody would have imagined college kids not drinking beer, but the data show that they are losing their taste for suds extremely rapidly, while wine is increasing in all demographics. Now, I cannot imagine Alpha Rho Gamma pounding cases of 1996 Saint-Emilion Premier Grand Cru at the homecoming party, but what is likely is that younger drinkers are starting with liquor and transitioning straight to wine as they get older. Not a good sign for brewers!

GLOBALIZATION

○ Retail volumes of beer in China rose 23.29 percent between 1997 and 2003, leading some analysts to conclude that there is potential for investment in that market.[9]

○ Chinese per capita beer consumption remains low compared to that in other Asian countries. In 2003, China remained at 18.76 liters per person, compared with 44.5 liters in South Korea, 41.9 in Japan, and 29 in Hong Kong.[10]

It appears that as China improves its standard of living and opens its doors to the world, it is steadily increasing its consumption of beer. It's not clear if economic success is the reason for the increased consumption of beer, but regardless the market is growing. It is always a good idea to consider the impact of the Chinese market when considering the future of *anything*. When a small percentage of a country with over a billion people starts doing anything more, it can change the dynamics of that industry. Clearly, we can conclude that the Chinese market for beer is increasing. Here's more evidence of how global activity influences the beer industry:

○ Beer marketing is becoming "multidimensional" for the major brewers due to globalization. Anheuser-Busch produced only 400,000 more barrels domestically, which represents a year of slow growth, but because of global market gains, top management may still view it as a good year. Budweiser's brand "may soon be as ubiquitous as Coca-Cola" overseas due to increases in sales in those new markets.[11]

By "multidimensional," *Modern Brewery* magazine means that American companies may need to focus on the marketing needs of multiple nations. Although growth in the American market is essentially flat, the real opportunity lies in the global market.

I have heard of Americans visiting Ireland expecting to see everyone drinking pints of Guinness, and instead shocked to see people in dance clubs pounding Budweiser and Bud Light. It could be that as breweries globalize, they may need to go wherever their brand is best known. Maybe one day Budweiser could be more popular in Ireland than it is in America.

PACKAGING

○ Widget cans, as used in packaging by Guinness, Tetley's, and other beers looking to deliver a draft experience, are improving the image of cans as packaging.[12]

In America, a six-pack (of cans) is considered "working class," whereas bottles that transport the expensive microbrews are thought to be more middle and upper class. However, widget cans, which make the beer froth when the can is opened, are actually bringing a kind of Euro chic to the aluminum can. Because cans are typically less expensive than bottles, this could affect the profit margins of beer companies in the future—you can impress your customers, and it will cost you less than glass!

BIOTECHNOLOGY AND AGRICULTURE

○ The fields of genomics, proteomics, and bioinformatics are decoding the genomes of malting barley, yeast, and hops— all of the major ingredients of beer.[13]

Because beer depends on agriculture, I had to check biotechnology to see if anything "cool" was on the way that would affect the beer industry. Unfortunately, the experts weren't saying much that was exciting. I could not collect enough data to suggest that this area will be big for beer in coming years. This is an example of a case where there were some data, but not enough to indicate a real trend. I know from studying biotechnology in researching past projects that genomic and proteomic research will allow scientists to understand disease pathways of these crops better. Maybe one day these insights will lead farmers to improve yield. However, nothing in the literature suggests a radical departure is imminent. I also searched several other sources, trying to find anyone who would comment on the role of biotechnology on the future of beer.

Again, I came up empty. It just doesn't seem to hold much promise for the brewing industry at this time.

This is a good example of real trend research. You can expect to run into some dead ends on subjects you at first think will be interesting. I guess biotechnology isn't going to produce any hangover-free beer. Damn.

MARKETING

o "Megatrends" according to the brewing industry:[14]

- A society where people "expect a lot more from their professional and private lives"

- Increased attention to health and diet

- Increased influence of women in society and the economy as a whole

- Increased focus on the aspirations and lifestyles of the Baby Boomer generation

o With the aggressive marketing of local breweries, distillers, and wineries, it is difficult to assign causes to the lack of growth in the traditional brewing segment. However, the "low-carb" craze is assumed to still have legs—Miller Lite's brand saw an estimated 600,000-barrel gain in 2004, even as Anheuser-Busch aimed to compete with Miller head-to-head.[15]

Health, diet, and women may explain why beer is losing out these days. It was strange to see beer companies fight over who had the lowest carb content during the Atkins Diet craze. Beer, despite some beneficial properties (and in my mind part of "the good life"), is not precisely a health tonic. The high carbohydrate content may have put beer in a losing position against wine and spirits, especially if women are making more of the decisions about what goes in the fridge. Ultimately, no beer company is an island:

○ Thony Ruys, former CEO of Heineken, recently said, "Ten years ago, our industry research was process oriented; today it starts more from the consumer end; for the future, we must be responsible and realize that one single company cannot undertake research projects alone on important general areas. Co-operation amongst companies is therefore essential on these projects."[16]

Ruys is getting the message—it's time to listen closer to a rapidly changing market segment. Listening to your customers isn't exactly new, but it is interesting to note that he talks about cooperation among companies. Remember that interconnection is not a zero-sum game, and even rivals may work together. It would be fascinating to know which projects he thinks the industry should undertake in the future. Maybe the companies will band together to deal with alcoholism or obesity. Maybe the larger trend here is that breweries are beginning feel under siege from falling market share and, therefore, feel the need to band together.

○ Peter V. K. Reid, editor of *Modern Brewery Age*, said, "Beer was once the first choice of the American working man. No beverage is as refreshing after hard physical work than a beer. But fewer Americans engage in hard, physical work. After a day at a desk, it may be that any sort of beverage will do."[17]

Aha! This fascinates me. Another key trend is the worldwide move away from manual labor toward knowledge work. More and more of the American economy is in the service sector—knowledge work that is valuable to other businesses. More Americans work behind a desk, not behind a lathe or in a steel plant or down on the farm. After a day in front of a computer screen, vodka might be just as good as beer. But after mowing lawns all day, vodka or merlot would be out of the question—and Budweiser tastes straight from heaven. There is no reason to think that the trend toward more knowledge work will lessen; if anything, more of our economy will become knowledge intensive. The archetype of the sweaty working American having a beer with the guys after work may be over. As the next data points suggest, beer consumption may be more of an experience than a beverage:

- Local craft brands have beaten down microbrewers that have sought national attention outside of their home territories. Pete's Brewing, a West Coast brewer, suffered a 15 percent drop in sales and was sold to Corona importer Gambrinus Company. Sales didn't rebound.

- According to Peter Egelston, president of Smuttynose Brewing Co. in Portsmouth, New Hampshire, "New England breweries will thrive in New England. Vermont and Maine in particular are very loyal to their own native-made products. Several years ago, West Coast breweries began sending their excess capacity out here and got their noses bloodied."[18]

- A new category of beer is emerging: "domestic imports." Rather than risk large shipping costs, broken bottles, and spoilage, foreign breweries are increasingly choosing to brew their beer under license at American facilities. Franconia Brewing Company, near Wilkes-Barre, Pennsylvania, is producing the crisp Bamberger Herren Pils under an agreement with the Keesman Brewery in Bamberg,

Germany. Pretzel City Brewery Company in Reading, Pennsylvania, is brewing and kegging Bolten Alt for the Bolten Brauerei in Dusseldorf, Germany.[19]

This is an interesting countertrend to the development of global brands. For a while there, it was looking like consumers would prefer giant, global brands recognized anywhere on earth. But this trend shows that people really prefer a taste of home, especially when it comes to beer. It's not that beer is completely unwanted. In fact, many consumers take it seriously, and want their beer to represent some part of their identity.

This trend gives us greater perspective on the growing success of microbreweries in the face of an overall flat beer market. Although it might appear that large breweries will enter the craft-brewing business to survive, this trend shows that the craft beer market is tougher than it first appeared. If large companies get into smaller brands of flavorful beer, they could be up against fierce competition from local breweries.

This research could go on forever. At some point, you have to take the trends you collect and build a view of the future. Let's recap the six trends we have so far uncovered about what is happening that will affect the future of beer.

- Beer consumption is falling in the U.S. compared with wine and spirits—especially in the critical youth market.

- As the world transitions to a knowledge economy and away from physical work, office workers could reach for vodka just as soon as beer.

- Beer is going global. China may soon be the world's biggest market for beer, and the Irish love Budweiser.

○ Beer is also local. In addition to national and global brands, consumers are growing more partial to locally made microbrews.

○ Packaging counts and can associate a brand's image with national pride as well as give it a certain status.

○ Trends in diet affect beer consumption as people attend closer to the health effects of alcohol intake.

What's next? Now that we have collected trend data, we need deeper insight. To get a vision of what the world will be like in 5 to 20 years, the next step is to collect and evaluate forecasts from the experts.

CHECKLIST: Analyzing Trends

✔ Start with the systems map you made. Use it to guide you to the trends you need to follow.

✔ Get acquainted with the topic through magazines and other popular media. Look for rigorous data in peer-reviewed journals, government reports, and in-depth business analyses.

✔ Don't expect the experts to tell you the future. They focus on reliable, specific data. You are the one who puts it together to form a broader picture.

WHAT YOU CAN DO TODAY

1. If you don't have five months to devote to trend collection, start small. Get a manila folder. Once a day, pick a trend area to look at: society, technology, economy, ecology, or politics. Look online and find one

interesting trend a day. After two months, you'll have 40 trends to guide you, all in just a few minutes a day.

2. To spread the work out even further, get a few colleagues to bring in their five favorite industry trends. With minimal effort, you'll collect dozens of trends to shape your research on the future, plus you'll lean more of what your colleagues think is important.

3. Start an online forum on trends. Invite colleagues to post future trends; then invite others to discuss the impact on them. This ensures that your company is more aware of just what is changing and how.

CHAPTER FOUR

into the future

making judgments;
evaluating forecasts

Using the best available trend data, you now know what is happening that will affect the future of the beer industry. You began your investigation by creating a systems map and conducting a search based on it in order to uncover various trends in consumption, retailing, global markets, and packaging. Trends alone are not enough; they only tell us what has happened up to now. To understand what *could* happen next, we need to project ourselves into the future. We need forecasts.

What Are Forecasts?

A forecast is a statement predicting what will happen in the future by a certain date: "By 2018, X will take place." For example, "By 2018, the personal computer will only cost $50," or "By 2018, we will be out of oil."

You can find forecasts in the same places you find trends: Experts comment on their fields and use their specific knowledge to tell you the date by which something might happen. For the above examples to be taken seriously, the forecasts need to come from people who have specific information; for example, someone who is involved in the design, manufacture, or marketing of computers for a major electronics firm or studies petroleum geology and oil reserves. Forecasting a date that is *not* based on knowledge is called "guessing."

Everybody loves forecasts. Executives believe they get to the heart of the matter, telling them how life—or at least a certain aspect of it—might change. For journalists, they are quotable and punchy! For everybody, forecasts make you think. It takes the future out of the abstract and makes it concrete. If you are like me, you can stop pondering the effects of a trend on the world and can rocket yourself into 2018 and take a look around, imagining exactly what will be different. Thanks to forecasts, I can imagine myself in the future, test that world out, and see how I like it. If I am thinking about what the vehicle of the future will be like and I read a forecast that says, "We'll be out of petroleum," then I have to imagine some other way to run a vehicle. No small task.

When you are trying to solve a problem relating to the future, you need to collect forecasts to get a real view of what it will be like. We are now entering a more dangerous, high-stakes world. Forecasts have power, and we must be responsible when employing them. The key is to *evaluate* the forecasts we collect. Not all of them carry equal weight! For example, compare the following three forecasts relating to the energy system in Europe:

1. By 2015, you will be able to buy either gasoline or hydrogen at most car-refueling stations in Europe.

2. Wind power will compose 10 percent of Europe's energy consumption by 2020.

3. The cost of biofuels will fall sharply around 2007 and will then account for 20 percent of European fuel needs.

These three statements are forecasts. Two of them come from world experts who have rigorously studied the future of European energy systems, and one I made up off the top of my head because it sounded plausible enough.

Can you tell which is which? Would you rely on all of these forecasts equally? That's the danger that comes from falling in love with every forecast you run into—not everybody uses equally good trend research from which to draw conclusions. There is a difference between the pontificator, the guesser, the amateur Nostradamus, and the subject-matter expert. Responsible futuring must be based on the best data available from experts, not simply personal biases and interesting reading. I have said that forecasting the future does not come from expert information alone. What that means is we don't rely on experts for our *entire* view of the future. However, nobody is better at interpreting what is coming in a specific area than those who spend their careers studying it. Go to the experts for their view of their field, and for those of you who don't have time or the resources to call experts, looking up their writing on Google works just as well. Combine several of these expert forecasts, and compare them. Now you have a superior view of the future that wasn't available anywhere else! (We will explore exactly how to do this in chapters 5 and 6.)

So, what about those three energy forecasts? The second and third came from a 2003 futures report by Risø National Laboratories in Roskilde, Denmark. Risø spent many months collecting data about the future of Europe's energy infrastructure, specifically exploring the future of renewable energy resources and the potential transition to a hydrogen economy when fuel cells come on line. From their data, they were able to generate forecasts about the consumption of wind power and biofuels. Thus, when properly cited, they are a reliable source. Of course, you need to bear in mind that they are not the *only* source, just one with credibility.

What about my "best guess" that hydrogen will be available at most European gas stations by 2015? I am not an expert on energy technologies and the development of the petroleum infrastructure in Europe. My *personal* guess, even if quite reasonable, even if likely to be correct, cannot carry the credibility of the experts. I might be right, but don't quote me.

Be aware—many people publish similarly poor forecasts. Such forecasts can gum up what you think about the future. Plenty of business gurus, journalists, and other analysts quote unreliable sources regularly when making forecasts. They try to sway opinion with sensational forecasts without revealing their biases or their sources. That's why you need to be able to tell the difference between a rigorously researched view of the future and someone's best guess. For forecasts, go to the experts!

One Forecast Is Good; More Are Better

If you are like most people, you are wondering about the future of a topic that is pretty broad. Let's say your field is health care, and you want to know what the doctor's office of the future will look like. Maybe you run a bowling alley, and you want to know what the future of sports and leisure will be. As you know from our discussion of systems thinking, there is a multitude of factors at play. Therefore, when collecting forecasts, you'll be searching out many experts from a variety of fields.

A few years ago, a client in the home-appliance field wanted to know what the kitchen of the future would look like so the client could think about how it might have to change its manufacturing or marketing practices. Based on our systems thinking, we knew that the kitchen is made up of lots of different factors and would be changed by many forces, including:

○ Home building

○ Materials

○ Families

○ Information technology

○ Manufacturing

Those were just a few of the major factors to explore. We began by looking at trends in home building. We went right to the experts. We contacted the National Association of Home Builders (NAHB) to find out what it was forecasting about the business of building homes. Its research showed that people would be increasingly concentrated in the suburbs surrounding urban areas but pushed farther from the city center. Because the drive time and the traffic would be getting worse in many cities, more people would be telecommuting. Because they would be home more often, they would be demanding more comfort and safety in the kitchen. As a result, the NAHB forecast that kitchens would require more information technology—"smart appliances," so to speak.

Remember, the association's forecasts were not necessarily going to be right. It too was just making an educated guess based on the best available data, but as a group of experts in the home-building industry, it was the best qualified to provide forecasts about such things as the size of the American kitchen in 2015 and what consumers were demanding in the way of technology and so on. However, when it came to discussing the specific information technologies that would be available for the kitchens of 2015, it too was out of its field.

Therefore, it was time to go to experts in information technology. We looked at trends in the specific technologies that would link up the kitchen of the future. We reasoned that computer processors and networks would be the key to kitchen electronics. There would be computerized devices, and these devices would somehow connect to either the Internet or internal networks. Therefore, we looked to the experts in these fields—semiconductor manufacturers, experts in Internet architecture, and members of the Consumer Electronics Association as well as the association itself. These member companies were the ones that would be making the products of the future, and they could tell us specifically what was coming down the line.

We learned about miniaturization and cheaper and more powerful wireless networks. Packaging would likely use radio-frequency ID tags to tell the fridge what it was. In other words, most of the devices would be talking to each other about what was in the kitchen. Most important, the home would run its own computer network, which would coordinate all of the devices in the home. Through IT, the smart home was on the way.

The final product was a series of scenarios that showed how the family of the future, informed by multiple expert forecasts, would use the kitchen of the future. Trends and forecasts indicated that the kitchen would be even more the center of the home than it already was and just as important to home health care as the bathroom. Many of the devices would work in a network, even able to know when the family needed more milk and bread—because the packages were talking to the fridge. Biosensors would pick up the odor of rotten food. The kitchen network would compare your food allergies with what was in the house and coordinate that information with any medications family members were taking (the medicine cabinet would also be digitized, which would help reduce errors).

Based on this information, our overall view of the kitchen of the future is that with all the technologies that will be available to it, it is likely that several kitchen devices will manage information to keep you and your family healthier and safer.

These forecasts were not available from any one expert. We had to combine the forecasts of many experts to derive a more complete view of the future. Experts will generally have a good idea of what the future of their own fields or industries will be like, but to envision its effects on you, you must combine multiple views.

Back to Beer: Forecasting the Future

To illustrate how you can use forecasts, let's go back to our test case, the future of beer. You will notice that there are typically fewer forecasts than trends. Typically, there are only so many experts willing to take a public stand, so the job of finding the opinions of the thought leaders is a little easier. I discovered these forecasts in the exact same places as I found the trend data—publications specializing in the brewing industry, such as *Modern Brewery Age* and *All About Beer*, as well as some articles from the Associated Press and even a report on agriculture from the provincial government of Alberta.

The experts underlined two major forecasts:

1. China will soon be the world's biggest market for beer.

2. As the youth market dissipates, future generations may not view beer as their favorite alcoholic beverage.

China I understand, but college kids not drinking beer—what kind of crazy talk is this? Let's look closer at the specific forecasts I uncovered for China:

○ China will soon be the world's largest beer market in terms of volume and growth.[1]

○ China is poised to overtake the United States as the world's number one beer market, to happen "sometime before the next century begins."[2]

Decision News Media published these forecasts from China's Brewing Industry Association. That's big news. However, the fact that American kids are turning away from beer while the Chinese are just warming up their taste buds could have serious implications for the industry. It is obvious that breweries need to consider exporting to China. It is not impossible that the major breweries will find themselves in a situation similar to the big tobacco companies, which are less concerned about antismoking laws in America because Asian markets are expanding so rapidly.

It is not, however, clear how the Chinese would translate "Miller Time." Consider what happened when the Kentucky Fried Chicken slogan "Finger Lickin' Good" became "Makes You Eat Your Fingers Off" in China. It was not a successful campaign. At this point, we can't be certain how American beer will play in China over the long term, but because it will be the world's biggest market for beer, advertisers should brush up on their Mandarin. Here's another forecast:

○ To really exploit the potential of genetic modification in beer, researchers will need to deepen their expertise in proteomics, finding the exact genotypes/phenotypes to modify and ultimately make barley, rice, and hops more hardy, nutritious, etc.[3]

This forecast comes from the provincial government of Alberta. Alberta grows a significant amount of grain for the brewing industry, so it is crucial for Alberta to know what will happen next in the industry. It is saying that to take real advantage of biotechnology, the brewing industry will need more data about the genetics of grain in order to make genetically modified versions of barley, rice, and hops that could be healthier and cheap to produce. The government agency didn't give any dates, but it said that the field needs more expertise before we will see any advances from biotechnology.

If you go back to Chapter 3, you will see I downplay the role of biotechnology in coming years. Even experts are hard-pressed to give dates when things will be different for beer because of biotechnology. If somebody took a chance and said, "By 2015, biotech will allow us to develop hardy crops of wheat that will grow anywhere, even in the desert, for 10 percent of the price of today's varieties," my ears would perk up and I would take notice. On the other hand, a vague forecast that someday proteomics and genomics (the science of genes and how they make proteins) will be important isn't exciting.

Drat. I was looking forward to someone telling me that genetic modification would mean that by 2014 we could have designed a beer to help us lose weight. The experts just don't see it. I guess I will just have to jog more.

Now here's a forecast about the effect of future generations on the beer industry:

○ Peter V. K. Reid, editor of *Modern Brewery Age*, said, "The next generation of drinkers may find martinis ridiculously fey and wine foolishly pretentious. But a generation is a long time to wait, so the big brewers had better start reinventing themselves now."

Mr. Reid has no trend data to suggest that drinkers will suddenly reject wine and spirits. If anything, the lack of acceptance of wine in America before the late 1990s has much more to do with the inexperience of American wineries; high tariffs on French wine; and the absence of up-and-coming producers in Chile, Australia, and New Zealand. Because the choice is available, there is little to support a forecast that makes a case for wine and spirits falling out of favor. Here is a supporting forecast:

○ In March 2005, the *Wall Street Journal* cited a Morgan Stanley survey suggesting that for the next five years sales of wine would rise 3.5 percent per year, sales of spirits would rise 2 percent, and beer sales would rise just 0.5 percent.[4]

This short-range forecast from the financial world supports the notion that the recent boom in wine and spirits is not just a fad. Beer will have strong competition for at least half a decade, possibly much longer. Although this was the only market forecast that was available, because it comes from Morgan Stanley, a source I have found very reliable, I tend to take it seriously. It will be advising people to invest in the beverage industry, and although I am not sure exactly how it arrived at this calculation, it lines up with the market trend research we conducted. Wine and spirits will likely take market share from beer as a result.

Putting the Data Together

Now that we can compare and contrast the opposing viewpoints of experts on a subject, it is time to put all these data together and look at how to determine the implications of all the data we have collected.

CHECKLIST: Forecasts

✔ Make sure you are getting forecasts from the best experts around. Know who the opinion leaders are in your industry. See what *they* think is going to happen. Check the keynotes at your professional conferences and look for other articles they have written.

✔ Check up on the experts! Because you also collect trends in other areas, make sure that any expert forecast lines up with other things going on in the world.

WHAT YOU CAN DO TODAY

1. When you look for trends in magazines, reports, and elsewhere, make sure to also look for forecasts. They usually have a date attached to them: 2015, 2020, 2030.

2. Keep a list of the most important forecasts from experts. You can make a time line using these dates—2010, 2015, 2020—which will help you see what the future might look like at a glance.

3. If the experts in your field have not published any forecasts, call them! Primary research like this can be just as effective as what you get from published sources.

strategic implications

what the future means to you

"So what? What if? What else?" Now that we have done the grunt work of futures research—collecting the best available trends and evaluating the forecasts of the world's experts—we need to be certain that we fully understand the *implications*: What exactly does all this research mean? The components of our study might be loaded with implications for the future, but after all that work is done, what are its implications for the top line? Is a crisis looming or an untapped opportunity begging for decisive action? What specifically might change? All futures analysis comes down to its applicability to today's decisions. Here are some questions to ask:

○ Does the future suggest we have new competitors who may take business from us? Are we no longer the only game in town?

○ Are the customers the same? Are there more or fewer customers?

○ Does this scenario suggest that new regulations are coming down the pike? Is there some public policy we should try to influence?

○ How will this future affect second- and third-world nations, as well as industrialized countries?

○ Are there any new liabilities waiting for us?

Without the ability to apply an analysis of the future to a strategic plan, futures research may still be entertaining—interesting to know what our kids might be facing when they run the world—but businesspeople need to make practical day-to-day, year-to-year decisions. To do this they must fully understand the implications—what their research truly means—for the future of their businesses.

Not All Implications Are Equal

Why must we spell out the implications of our research even to ourselves? Aren't they obvious? There are a couple of answers to this basic question.

First, no, implications are not always obvious. The majority of people in an organization might be reading about trends and might be tracking some specific changes, but that won't necessarily lead to an understanding of what the future will hold. It isn't until all the information is together—until it is superconnected—that the threats and opportunities become evident.

Think about it. Most leaders I know read several newspapers, news magazines, and industry trade tabloids, and they attend several conferences a year. They have significant human intelligence networks, people at all levels of their industry they can turn to and from whom they can get the latest industry news. Even small-business owners have subscriptions to *Economist* and *BusinessWeek* to keep current.

Second, implications by their nature may suggest that some sort of shake-up is in the offing. They may even be threatening prophecies! Some of us prefer the ostrich approach; others tend to see the future in rosier terms and view forecasts of systemic change as overblown or exaggerated.

Deciphering the Real from the Spurious

Not every implication is really about "The Future."

Implications are "the good stuff" of futures work, but understanding what they mean and which are "real" is not always easy. It takes a little practice and a little skill. That's why not all reports claiming to tell you about The Future provide useful information.

At many conferences, you'll find some keynote speech, breakout session, or workshop on the future of the _____ industry. Come hear about the future of food safety! The future of pharmaceuticals! The future of baseball! Chances are what you hear at these sessions contains more information about the present than the future. That is because identifying implications is tricky business, and many presenters do not have the benefit of a rigorous futures methodology. They fall back on "conclusions" and "implications" that are not really about the future.

Here are three classic "implications" you should not take seriously:

1. TOMORROW WILL BE MORE COMPETITIVE THAN EVER

This is a classic. Useless, but classic. Any student of history knows that humans are pretty competitive. The less competitive are stomped on. Athens and Sparta were pretty competitive. The Maori islanders beat up on other less competitive Polynesians. During the first wave of conquest, the Spanish and the Portuguese were at each other's throats in every way possible, but especially economically. In the nineteenth century, the British economy competed with just about everyone. Back in the 1980s, the Japanese juggernaut was fiercely gnawing at our steel; semiconductor; and, of course, automobile industries. Do you really believe that at any time in history people were just sitting on their butts? The notion that yesterday's business environment was placid and wonderful, like a weekend at your fishing camp; that today is normal; and that tomorrow will be *ultracompetitive* is useless and even dangerous.

To say that competition will come from unlikely places, such as El Salvador, rather than Germany, is interesting. Simply saying competition will be tougher is not. The ambitious have been looking to get ahead throughout civilization, and there are thousands of historical anecdotes to prove it.

Competition is only an interesting implication when it changes suddenly and fundamentally—like an exponential growth in competitors because the capital equipment required for entry fell to the point where small and medium businesses could afford it. In music, professional recordings can now be made with $1,000 in equipment, whereas previously it took $100,000 to cut an album in a studio. That's an implication. When you can get into the steel industry with a small-business loan of only $300,000, as opposed to $300 million, now we're talking radical new competition. Don't just tell me—or yourself—that tomorrow's competitor is going to be "fiercer." Ask why it will be fiercer.

2. IN THE FUTURE, WE WILL BE MORE EFFICIENT. STREAMLINING IS KEY!

Here is another nonstarter. Wow, you say the future will be more efficient; the future is all about streamlined processes. No, it's not. That implication comes from a mind that cannot grasp the future. It essentially says that tomorrow will be just like today, only a little quicker. History tells us that all technical and social changes ensure greater efficiency. Steam power was more efficient than water power. Mass production was more efficient than handicrafts. That's a characteristic of all economic activity—to achieve greater profits from streamlined processes.

For that reason, efficiency by itself is not much of an implication—but definitely give me a call when you are about to shave 90 percent off production time or triple the speed of research and development. When you are talking about the future of pharmaceuticals, let me know when all of a sudden the time it takes to develop a drug drops from 15 years to 5 years; then the strategists will have something to worry about. On the other hand, when everyone in the company gets the latest version of Microsoft Office and thus shaves three months off the total time it takes to develop and launch a product due, that is not nearly as interesting.

3. THIS NEW GADGET MEANS THE FUTURE IS ACTUALLY HERE!

I have heard this one enough times that I actually wanted to rush to the podium and hit the speaker with a rubber chicken. The future is *not* now. Now is now. The future is later, and these days it is probably going to be weirder than we can imagine. I never want to hear that because of some miracle innovation "the future is already here."

I remember attending a conference on food safety where in a breakout session discussing the future one of the speakers displayed her company's products to show how the future was ensuring more control of bacteria in chicken processing . . . *TODAY!* That's right folks; you can streamline your processes and make sure you are in regulatory compliance with today's technology! No need to wait.

This was offensive on several levels. Not only was it gauche for her to speak to an audience of her peers and use it as an opportunity to sell, but, more important, the speaker was so entranced by her product that she seemed unable to imagine any technologies that would be available in 10 years to change the food production industry, that is, the actual future. In fact, questions from the audience about the role of biotechnology in the food industry were met with blank stares and more sales pitches about the implications of today's technologies.

People are often so entranced by how much has changed during their careers that they hesitate to imagine further changes. This is why many people spend their time looking at the deeper implications of the changes of the last 10 years. This is not without value; you need to know what has already happened, but it is equally important to consider what we are going to do with all of today's technologies—how are they still changing us. There is so much going on right now, and we are still feeling the strategic impact of past innovations that it is very useful to consider the *tactical* implications of the next few years on technological changes to our industries.

This is another reason why in studying the future your time frame should range from 5 to 20 years. If you start examining the next one to five years, you will probably be sucked into a tactical discussion and be dissuaded from exploring fundamental *strategic* changes. There is nothing wrong with exploring the near term—tactics are how we actually make money and execute today's policies—but if it's a strategic decision, you should be looking five or more years into the future, out to a place beyond your comfort zone, but where you can let your imagination have more power. Also, if you run a small business, 5 to 20 years in the future is likely when you plan to sell your business and retire. Your life of well-earned leisure is at stake.

Now that we know what implications *aren't*, let's look at the tools we need to discover what they *are*.

Tools for Extracting the "Real" Implications

This is the dramatic, fun part, where we take the special knowledge gathered from your study and find new ways to combine it to see if some threat or opportunity looms. The excitement comes from uncovering knowledge that may not have been obvious without this kind of study. With this new knowledge, you can prepare a vigorous response rather than a haphazard one.

This is the creative part, certainly, but it is based on a methodology that ensures consistency from project to project.

The Futures Wheel

Jerry Glenn, head of the United Nations University Millennium Project and author of *State of the Future*, was just a graduate student when he gave this tool to the futures community—a visual of a wheel showing how one change, one driver, one trend, one technology is so interconnected that it changes the future of everything around it.

The real usefulness of the Futures Wheel is that it shows the many layers of implications inherent in every change. The primary implications are the most obvious—changes that occur specifically because of the driver being analyzed. However, those secondary and tertiary changes are the ones that sneak up on us.

My favorite example of multiple implications is the impact that the mass production of automobiles had. For example, it:

○ Kept me from knowing my grandparents well

○ Put about 10 pounds on my gut

○ Helped my high school classmates have sex

How? Let's explore how you go from the car to obesity and teen sex by looking at Figure 5–1.

Look how multiple levels of implications stem from any one development. The introduction of the automobile to modern society leads to families that are more isolated, obesity, and a change in sexual behavior. How?

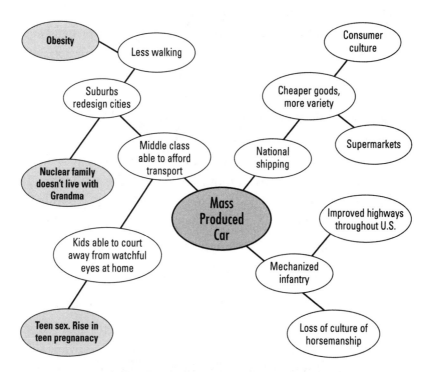

FIGURE 5–1. Futures wheel: implications of the mass-produced car.

1. THE MASS-PRODUCED AUTOMOBILE LOOSENED FAMILY TIES

The car loosened family ties because it came at a time when multiple generations of families lived together, often under the same roof. Married couples, babies, kids, and grandma and/or grandpa likely lived in the same house, offering support, sharing wisdom, cooking meals together (and, if modern sensibilities have any connection to the past, probably driving everybody a little bit crazy). For thousands of years, we grew up under the watchful eyes of our elders in small, dense pedestrian cities or with our family members in far-flung farming communities. No technologies really changed this pattern for millennia.

Enter the mass-produced automobile and a well-constructed road system to match. Suddenly, especially in America, city planning changed dramatically. With reliable cars affordable by many, you could get to work on time from places farther away. Add to this the swelling population of the postwar nation, and the result was cities that grew to include *suburbs*. Finally, the stresses between sons and mothers-in-law, or tension simmering between mothers and daughters-in-law, could be defused as cheap land became accessible away from the city center.

This led to the nuclear family, for the first time just mom, dad, and the kids. No grandma in sight—she could finally afford her own place. This glut in real estate made possible by the car gave older couples their privacy. Visits to grandma's became events, as young people were now typically separated from daily contact with their elders.

2. THE AUTOMOBILE LED TO SEDENTARY LIFESTYLES

Prior to the notion of "a car in every garage," people either lived within walking distance to their workplaces (or schools) or they were not far from a train, trolley, or bus that would carry them part of the way. Today, as more of us live in the suburbs or in the "exurban" countryside outside of cities, we can expect one to three hours a day in our cars, depending on the number of errands we run or where we work.

Talk about building machines to ensure a sedentary life—the interior of a well-appointed Lexus SUV has comfy leather seats, multizone climate control, a nice sound system, and even a DVD player. It's nicer than some living rooms.

Therefore, mass-produced cars = suburbs = more time commuting = less walking = I should lay off the barbeque chips if I want to lose those 10 pounds.

3. THE MASS-PRODUCED AUTOMOBILE LED TO UNPRECEDENTED PRIVACY, EVEN FOR TEENS

When mass-produced automobiles infiltrated the middle class, for the first time in history, technology provided the means for teenagers to speed away from the watchful eye of their elders. Consider how the automobile altered American courtship rituals. The notion of courting a girl on the porch became antiquated, and the modern notion of "the date" evolved. The car gave teenagers privacy for the first time in history. Hence, the sexual connotation of the phrase "in the backseat."

Secondary and Tertiary Implications in Action: The PC

A key concept is the idea of secondary and tertiary implications, second- and third-order effects of trends or events. Because the world is superconnected, nothing changes just one aspect of life; the effects ripple out. Many people consider the first level of change but don't look deeper. Being a good strategic planner involves thinking beyond the obvious impact of change to see just how life could be different in its broadest sense.

To see how this kind of thinking works, let's examine the impact of cheap transistors and the deeper impact of the personal computer on our lives.

TREND DRIVER: SMALLER, CHEAPER TRANSISTORS

- *Primary Implication:* Desktop computer invented

- *Secondary Implication:* Word processing available on every desk, more executives expected to communicate using desktop

- *Tertiary Implication:* "Typing pools," generally composed of women, became a thing of the past; not simply drudges in the workplace; freer to progress up the ladder of success in a knowledge economy

We know the story of the computer chip and that it ultimately changed business, but, through the lens of multiple levels of implications, watch how one technology changes how society behaves. Consider what the desktop computer really meant for business around the world.

The desktop computer isn't just important for bringing processing power to companies—mainframe computers had been doing that for years. Their real impact was elsewhere. Desktop computers led executives to type their own letters and memos, making typing pools an anachronism, which led to changes in the role of women in the workplace. No longer relegated to typing all day, but still a basic part of office life, women were free to take on roles of greater responsibility, moving the office a step further away from the Old Boys' Club.

Without question, the increased role of women in the workplace was also due to 100 years of universal suffrage, the role of women during World War II, and feminism. The personal computer, word-processing software, and MS-DOS removed one last vestige of women working purely as administrative drudges. Today, as global economies are more about knowledge than dragging sheet steel around a factory, the role of women is increasing in many industries.

This brings us back to the concept of interconnection. The implications of a new technology go far beyond the initial market for that technology because the world is interconnected. It's also why good futures analysis depends on a rigorous examination of both technological and social trends—the trends tend to shape each other. New technologies change how people behave, and changed people tend to seek new technologies.

Think about it. Why, for example, would someone develop a Blackberry handheld e-mail device if executives all relied on their secretaries to do the typing? First, there had to be the "emancipation" of the executive to write his or her own letters with a PC, then e-mail communications took over for letters and memos, and only then did telecommunications companies develop the Blackberry. It is difficult to envision the development of such a device if you remain stuck on the idea, "You don't understand; executives aren't like that. They depend on their administrative assistants to write for them."

YOU TRY IT: USING THE FUTURES WHEEL

So let's try a Futures Wheel ourselves, using a "wild-card event"—something that is unlikely, but with high impact—as the basis for this exercise: What are the primary, secondary, and tertiary implications of a sudden increase in the price of gas to US$10 per gallon in the United States?

Let us imagine that several factors converge to slash the supply of oil to the United States: Hurricanes take out the Gulf Coast petroleum infrastructure, America is in an armed conflict with Venezuela, and Saudi Arabia begins to divert much more of its production to China. A "perfect storm" of factors work to make the average price of a gallon of regular unleaded $10 at the pump. What are the far-reaching implications, beyond the first level of reactions? We know that prices will go up for goods that need to be shipped (almost everything) and that people will likely start carpooling. We know that Detroit will start making smaller cars and that perhaps the salesperson at the Hummer dealership will be lonely.

What are the implications for pharmaceuticals if gas prices shoot through the roof? How about real estate agents? A group of business students at American University did this exercise. You would think they worked for petroleum industry think tanks, given their insightful responses:

- Real estate prices would increase in downtown areas—commuting gets expensive!

- There would be more public transportation, even for the upper middle classes—the bus will no longer have a "working-class" air about it.

- French "Smart Cars" would be imported (these anti-SUVs would make golf carts look like M1 tanks).

- There would be less obesity from increased walking.

Cross-Impact Analysis

The Futures Wheel is great, but what if you have many different trends to deal with and you want to do a rigorous analysis? If you don't want to miss details, a chart technique called cross-impact analysis is a way to make sure you take every trend seriously and look for unique combinations that might otherwise escape you. Let's look at the future of cereal production.

	Increased processing power	Increasing globalization of cereals production	Aging population
Increased processing power	X		
Increasing globalization of cereals production		X	
Aging population			x

This tool makes you check every trend, forecast, or wild-card against every other one uncovered in the course of your analysis. In the above example, you will be forced to consider:

Increased processing power + Global cereals production = ???

Increased processing + Aging population = ???

Global cereals production + Aging population = ???

Some of these combinations may not yield brilliant insights, as the aging populations may not have much to do with wheat production in Mongolia. (What if retirees could do high-tech farming? It might not be a strange combo after all.) Don't be constrained by analyzing only global issues. These techniques work just as well for the tactical details of your business. The point is that you want to expand your thinking so you consider possibilities of all kinds. The future is usually stranger than we expect it to be, so it pays to start with weird combinations.

Structure Your Thinking

Reading something about the future that has clear strategic implications for your business can leave you saying, "This changes *everything*." Of course, it won't help to think you have to change "everything." You can't suddenly do that. That is why it is important to have a filter for evaluating implications.

Now, go back to STEEP analysis. It's a simple, easy-to-remember structure for examining what something means.

Society—Will this affect people? What about family structure? Will work life change?

Technology—Does this development imply that a new technology will become available? Will it eclipse an existing technology? Increase the market for other technologies? How will R&D need to react?

Economics—Will this change most businesses? How about governments—will they need to alter their fiscal policies? Will consumers act differently as a result?

Ecology—What are the implications for the natural systems that support us? Will this change reduce the impact of human activity on the ecosystem? Will it cause a new stress? Does this change represent the tipping point that will make us see the damage being done to ecosystems?

Politics—How will this driver change governance? Will it alter election dynamics? Change the type of leadership? Will new groups begin to exert force on the government?

Now that you are able to think systemically, collect trends, evaluate expert forecasts, and fathom the implications of your discoveries, you can assemble scenarios that tell the real story.

CHECKLIST: Implications

✔ Now that you know which trends are most important, ask, *So what? What if?* and *What else?* Don't just settle for interesting data; ask yourself specifically how the change could affect your business.

✔ Focus especially on the potential customers, competitors, and new technologies. The implications to worry about are the ones so big it will take time to affect the appropriate change in your company.

✔ Avoid incremental thinking about implications. Look beyond simple conclusions such as, "the world will be more competitive." Thing big, think strange!

✔ Go back to your STEEP thinking when interpreting the impact of trends. Think about how trends and forecasts will change society, technology, economics, ecology, and politics. Don't just think about your own situation; think broadly.

✔ Use tools such as the Futures Wheel and cross-impact analysis to make sure you are thinking broadly and about the interconnection of lots of trends.

WHAT YOU CAN DO TODAY

1. Implications are really a team sport. Once you have your trends and forecasts collected, figuring out what it means depends on a variety of personalities and experiences. If you're a small business, you may be on your own, or need to consult a trusted adviser. For larger groups, collect your trend data in one place and give it to a group of 5 to 10 people to get impressions of what the strategic effects could be.

2. The Futures Wheel is a great way to lead meetings about implications. Make your own wheel, put a trend or forecast in the center, and then ask your team to work together on what will be changing. Ask your colleagues to look at first-, second-, and third-order effects. Society and technology count equally here!

3. If you want to dive deeper, put together a big chart for cross-impact analysis. Take a large piece of poster paper, and chart all of your trends. Write down how they interact on an individual basis. This is one way to get hundreds of strategic insights all in one place. Leave it up next to the coffeemaker and generate some discussions about what's next.

CHAPTER SIX

scenario
generation

drawing a picture
of the future

N ow you now know what is coming, and, through your analysis of implications, you know more about what it means. However, implications are abstract concepts that are useful in developing strategy. You can list and even explain them to others and tell them exactly what to look out for, but this doesn't always make an impression.

Actually, that makes sense. Which is better: a list of implications about the future of packaging technology or the following description?

    May 12, 2017. Around breakfast time.
    Anytown, USA:

> Because today's milk bottles are made
> from a self-sterilizing, self-cleaning
> nanomaterial, we never throw them away;
> we always take the bottle back to the
> store. It saves us a buck. Plus, the
> Fresh-Sense™ coating on the interior
> glows blue when the milk is turning, so
> we always know if it's bad before we
> pour it on our cereal.

There's a significant amount of data packed in that little vignette, which is based on forecasts about nanotechnology, materials science, sustainability, information technology, retailing, and food. Just making a list of trends about those six sectors is important, but for many of us, it doesn't catch our attention until we can put it all together into a simple, clear, well-founded scenario showing how people will act in the future.

Abstract is good, but a quick scene about how in 2021 there are three times as many competitors in your industry, requiring you to merge with your biggest rival in order to survive—that's more bracing than a strong cup of espresso.

Draw a Mental Image

If you present chunks of data, even about a topic someone cares about, frequently the person will soon forget those bits of data. However, a good story, one with memorable characters, maybe even a funny punch line—that's something that people can walk away with and tell their friends. Stories are the most powerful communication tool we have. According to neuroscientists and developmental psychologists, we are able to start writing analytically, on average, by age eight, whereas there is evidence to suggest that children are able to start telling narrative stories to themselves and others by age *two*. The ability to refer important information to other humans through a narration appears to be deeply imbedded in what it means to be human. To communicate our ideas about the future to our colleagues, we must master the ability to do it in a way that doesn't get lost in the cloud of other minutiae they must remember.

Let's take the looming crisis in health care as an example of how scenarios can communicate a situation more powerfully than data alone. To begin, the following is one way you might present trends that will affect the future of health care, in no particular order:

○ The cost is increasing.

○ The Baby Boomers will be the largest group of people over 65 in American history.

○ The Indian middle class is growing.

○ Outsourcing overseas is increasing as a strategy to keep costs low.

○ Diagnostic equipment is falling in price and is increasingly connected to the Internet.

Let us say that you put this list in front of the senior VP of strategy at your company. Do you think she will jump out of her chair? I'll bet she will mix it up with all the other observations about the world she has to deal with, because there's nothing there that will keep her from thinking about more immediate concerns, like implementing the launch of the latest piece of equipment. Work at a small company? Your boss will likely say the same thing. There's no wow factor, yet. These are interesting observations, but the information by itself is so abstract that it isn't useful as a strategic tool.

However, when the trends are crafted into a scenario of the future, a story jumps out:

> 2013: America, fiscally burdened by the cost of its massive retired population, begins to outsource some health care duties to doctors in India. "Telemedical" remote diagnostic machines, located in American clinics, take readings to document a patient's symptoms and vital signs. Much of the mundane work of the primary care physician is outsourced using the Internet, although tough cases are still referred to American specialists. Thousands of American health care jobs are lost, but costs are finally being cut and health care outcomes are at least as good as before.

Now *that* story should give health care executives something to ponder. When translated into a story, the trend data takes on a life of its own. It is no longer about abstract concepts; it generates curiosity. When reading a story about other people (or companies or nations), curiosity is almost instantly piqued because the story challenges our assumptions about the people of the future. Instead of a ho-hum response, it elicits provocative questions such as:

○ What do you mean, "America is fiscally burdened"? How bad?

○ Is telemedicine really a big deal? When did it get important?

○ Could foreign countries compete in our health care market—*from abroad?*

○ How many jobs are being lost overseas? Does that affect our economy even further?

Though it may not turn out exactly like that in 2013, the implications of that story *as it develops* will change how the executive thinks about the coming competitive pressures on the industry. Now there are specific questions to track:

○ Is globalization going to affect the American hospital?

○ Are we investing enough in innovative information technologies? What about our competitors?

○ Will foreign medical students who come to America stay, or will they be better able to practice in their home countries?

○ How much pressure is the retirement of the Baby Boomers going to put on health care practices? Can we minimize the discomfort by planning for it?

These are essential questions, and it's the story that gets the message across.

BRING SCENARIOS TO LIFE WITH DETAILS

Scenarios are especially powerful when we make them about *people* instead of trends. Trends are abstract observations about how the world is changing. A TV show about abstract trends would bomb in the ratings, but scenarios about individuals in the future making decisions based on all the constraints of their lives can be engaging. When we visit people out where they live, in the future, we get a chance to look around and really think about what their assumptions about life are, to see if anything has changed.

One of the tricks is to show the reader what is "normal" in the future. Futurist Joe Coates talks about his old trick of thinking about the burglar of the future to explore the future of crime or of the house:

> I ask myself, what would a burglar be going through if he was robbing a house in 2018? How did he get into the house? Are there sophisticated security systems, such as motion detectors? Are they cheap enough for anyone to buy? What kinds of goods will be available then? Are televisions outdated, having given way to built-in wall plasma screens? Will it be possible to steal them and sell them at the fence? Has the police force become any more sophisticated about catching criminals, so that burglary is a very risky proposition?[1]

Two things happen when you put yourself in the shoes of the burglar of the future. First, you must consider the superconnection among all the trends you have studied and think deeply about all the ways the home of the future will interact with different changes in the world. Second, you must consider all the assumptions that the burglar of the future has. What does he find commonplace? What would be old-fashioned? What is very new?

We think about the burglar of the future to escape one of the biggest traps we can fall into when thinking about the future—assuming that people in the future will think about life exactly as we do. Every generation thinks different facets of life are "normal" in ways that would make previous generations wonder how we could even belong to the same species. Just imagine the shocking things we, in the United States, find normal that our grandparents would find strange:

○ Women regularly work outside the home.

○ People of different religions often marry without causing riots.

○ World travel on aircraft is fairly commonplace for the middle class.

○ Owning three cars isn't impossible for a middle-class family of three.

Think about how many decisions we make differently than our grandparents did because of these assumptions. Vacation in Paris even though you are a schoolteacher: Why not? Buy your son a car so he can get around easier: No reason not to. Remember, it would have been an unthinkable future to your grandparents when they were growing up. Perhaps this explains why they have always looked at us kind of funny.

Don't forget that these attitudes about the future apply going forward as well as looking back; future generations will make different decisions based on the constraints and freedoms of their lives, not ours. Some goods will be cheaper, others more expensive. Some experiences will be commonplace, others a reminder of a distant past. Don't get caught in the trap of assuming that future generations will think as you do.

ROLE PLAYING BRINGS THE FUTURE HOME

Even in live settings, not just reports, making a scenario come to life through individual characters makes the future more vivid for all involved. Executives from a semiconductor company were asked to role-play about the work lives of different people on different continents; each executive got a different role to play.

As luck would have it, the man asked to play a 14-year-old boy from Qatar, raised in a conservative Muslim family, was the most conservative person in the group. He was asked to imagine himself inside the mind of this boy, watching the headlines today, living the life of a modern Muslim affected by globalization just as we all are, and imagine how that young man might look for work and how it would affect his family life.

Given a three-by-five-inch card with the boy's vital statistics and cultural assumptions written on it, the executive really inhabited the boy's life, explaining how this boy was likely to be a breadwinner for the family soon, did not hate Western countries or their corporations, and might consider working for a company that moved to Qatar. He explained how the boy had to balance his job prospects with his duty to family and to Allah, giving specific reasons why he might support or object to Western business in the area. It was fascinating to watch someone who probably had not thought deeply about how modern Muslims make their decisions. But after stepping into the person's shoes, he suddenly understood exactly what it was to balance family, religion, and commerce from an Islamic perspective.

Applying a Scenario

Choose your own adventure—construct an alternative future to understand all the available options. It is important to understand that creating scenarios cannot just be about putting information into one plausible story about the future. That's because we can't actually know the future (which is obvious, really), and so to pretend that there is one future more likely than any other is very dangerous. After all, if you are wrong about key details, and that's likely in a fast-paced world, then people may think you are a fraud at worst, mistaken and unreliable at best.

The point is not that there is one future, but that there are *multiple alternative futures*, a number of scenarios constructed from the trends driving change in the world. By knowing the potential futures, we can then make smarter choices for our organizations and ourselves. Moreover, these decisions based on multiple scenarios change how we make decisions, and thus change the future. It is a constant feedback loop between looking at the future and changing it.

Avoid Pollyannaism: Consider the Alternatives

Wait! I can write a scenario of the future my bosses will love. This is one reason why multiple scenarios are necessary. In many organizations, there is a tremendous temptation to look at a variety of trends and combine them into a comfortable vision of the future, especially a *normative* future where everything works out okay. Perhaps you have seen this type of future scenario in a vision statement for a company:

```
2020: Through ingenuity and diligence,
ACME Corporation has become first-in-
class in its industry, burying all rivals,
and delighting the world with a variety
of products and services, providing
value to all stakeholders. ACME has
learned to master globalization, a
changing workforce, new competitors,
retirement of most of its senior staff
back in 2013, and some major historical
events to become one of the world's most
esteemed companies.
```

Sounds great, doesn't it? In this loosely constructed scenario, the company envisions a future in which it masterfully met all the challenges. Nobody will get in trouble for posting this scenario in the break room.

This kind of scenario generation is useless, unless it is thought of as a vision statement. Any useful study involves *multiple* views of the future: some positive, some undesirable, some completely marginal and unsurprising, and others that ponder what life would be like if some wild-card event took place. This is called the theory of alternative futures, originally advanced by Herman Kahn of the RAND Corporation, a think tank that works closely with the Pentagon.

The value of having multiple future scenarios is twofold:

1. They communicate a large amount of trend data in an easy-to-digest story format.

2. They present multiple stories that show how the prevalence of different trends could make the future go a number of different ways.

All scenarios should be constructed based on multiple trend areas—in other words, don't just make one change at a time, for example, custom-made plastics or free telephone service; show your audience (or yourself) a world where many things have changed. This illustrates the effects of superconnection and demonstrates the depth of trend research. For example, when you write a scenario about the future of air travel, you unveil trends in:

○ Aircraft (How are we flying?)

○ Economics (Do people have more money to travel?)

○ Food packaging (What kinds of food can be delivered, hot and fresh, to passengers?)

○ Materials science (Are the seats any more comfortable?)

These are the trend data you are trying to detail. In a scenario about these trends, you might tell a story about a middle-class family in New Delhi in 2024 boarding a microairframe shuttling 50 people from India to San Francisco. The shuttle serves fresh, delicious vegetarian dishes. In this way, you are able to synthesize all your research in one elegant phrase.

Scenarios at Work: Broad and Focused

There are multiple ways to write scenarios to present different points of view. Sometimes leaders need to see the broadest possible trends. In other situations, industry-specific detailed views are more helpful. Here are some examples.

BROAD SCENARIOS

Typically, broad scenarios are better for large issues, such as questions about how to position a company or agency strategically for the long term. Larger questions go beyond today's competitors to wider concerns, such as:

○ Are we ready for a Gen X client base? In addition, are we prepared to recruit our employees from that generation? What do we have to offer?

○ Can we handle eventual competitors from China and India?

○ Will Africa eventually modernize to the point that it will have a significant middle-class market? Should we begin investing early to beat our competitors?

These broad scenarios give a larger sense of where the world is headed. Consider a study titled *Great Transitions: The Promise and Lure of Times Ahead* by the Stockholm Environment Institute and its Global Scenario Group. This study explored multiple social and economic trends to show a number of ways that our globally integrated economy could develop. The researchers started with the assumption that human endeavor has reached a new era—a planetary phase where all activities on the globe are integrating into a planetary culture. According to the authors, variances in many of the raw trends studied could result in dramatically different scenarios.

The result of the study is a group of broad views about the direction of the future:

The *Conventional Worlds* view forecasts a world that in 20 years looks significantly like our own—nothing dramatically different. In the Conventional Worlds scenarios, the global system will progress without major surprises, sharp discontinuities, or a fundamental transition in the bases of human civilization. For example, a scenario called *Market Forces* showed the status quo where corporations are the most important drivers of the future. Another scenario, *Policy Reform*, showed that same world relying on government policies to drive future prosperity.

The *Barbarism* view offered two scenarios depicting a world where violence and economic insecurity weaken social systems. In *Breakdown*, government and economic institutions begin to collapse as conflict and crises spiral out of control. *Fortress World* shows a similarly desperate situation, but one where the rich live in enclaves surrounded by the poor and ruled by strong leaders.

The *Great Transitions* view (after which the whole study was named) supposes that we take the global pressures on our society and make a leap to a creative renaissance that transforms all society. In *Eco-Communalism*, people organize social systems focused around ecological sustainability, local democracy, and economic self-sufficiency. Small but beautiful once again becomes the slogan. In *New Sustainability Paradigm*, world societies will grow together through global solidarity, communication between cultures, and economic integration.

This kind of scenario work is ideal for people wondering where their place in history is. Many leaders today believe that major transitions are under way, and a study like this provides detailed reasons for why the world *could* evolve in different ways. We talked earlier about the phenomenon of companies preferring to believe that a positive future for their business is on the way (a future that is, naturally, good for stockholders). In the world of global economic development, a similar status quo mind-set is a tempting trap.

FOCUSED SCENARIOS

Focused scenarios usually answer specific questions, such as, How could a certain trend play out, and who will profit the most? A focused scenario will ask more specific questions, for example:

○ What will happen if American companies do not embrace IPv6 fast enough, and Europe or Asia becomes the leader of the next Internet?

○ What might happen if gasoline is $7 a gallon in 2009?

○ What might Pennsylvania do without its steel industry?

Although the view from 50,000 feet is interesting for thinking about the grand questions, there are tools to drill into more specific scenarios. Whether your business is large or small, you need to consider different views of the future specific to your situation. Questions such as, Will global prosperity lift Africa, too? are important for all, but they are so broad that they aren't especially useful to any one industry. On the other hand, ask something short-term and focused, such as, What might the pharmaceutical industry look like if companies are forced to report all of their clinical trials to a public database? and the heads of all the pharmaceutical executives in the room will turn.

For example, scenario analysis was recently a very useful tool in guiding a number of drug company executives to recognize a shift that could destabilize the nature of competition in their industry.

The Impact/Probability Matrix

When you present several scenarios, it is useful to think of them in terms of their relative likelihood and impact on the industry, as not all scenarios are as probable or as drastic. One effective tool for scenario development is the Impact/Probability Matrix. The matrix presents four potential scenarios and compares each scenario's potential impact and probability. To use the matrix correctly, it is important to understand these terms:

- *Impact* is the estimation of whether a trend could be mildly disruptive, requiring a few new practices, or disturbing, perhaps even requiring a change of business altogether.

- *Probability* is a measurement of how likely a scenario is and what events would bring it about.

This tool is useful for several reasons. It is a quick way to develop four individual scenarios with different implications for the organization. Four is a good number because the number of scenarios presented affects how your colleagues react.

○ *Two* creates a football match mentality—our side or theirs.

○ *Three* lets people choose a middle ground, an often falsely moderate position.

○ *Five or more* can be confusing and difficult to understand.

○ *Four* is perfect because it gives a range of possibilities with no middle option.

You must consider and choose. It doesn't give you an easy way out. For this reason, the Impact/Probability Matrix produces several scenarios with distinctly different characteristics. Figure 6–1 illustrates one way to structure scenarios in the matrix.

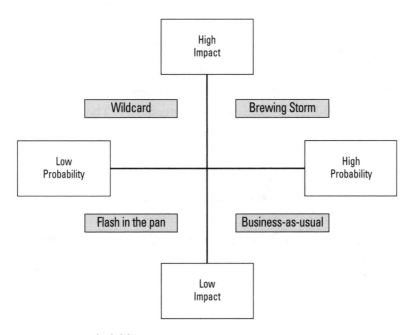

FIGURE 6–1. Impact/probability matrix.

LOW PROBABILITY, LOW IMPACT—FLASH IN THE PAN

This scenario shows a future that could turn out to have little disruption and, thus, any overreaction would be wasted energy. This scenario is often premised on the idea that the coming change will not be a big deal or that it will blow over quickly.

HIGH PROBABILITY, LOW IMPACT—BUSINESS AS USUAL

A change is coming, but we can adjust to it without any major growing pains. We need to observe the forces at play to see if some things will change, but our business will remain fundamentally unchanged.

HIGH PROBABILITY, HIGH IMPACT—THE BREWING STORM

This is often what executives focus on most, a scenario signaling a real problem. You can see the path of this brewing storm, and an exploration of this future will point to signs we need to watch for.

LOW PROBABILITY, HIGH IMPACT—WILD CARD

Wild cards are those scenarios that are unlikely but could arrive if a couple of events come in rapid succession and change everything. It's the blindside, the "We never saw it coming." The stars would really need to line up, but if they did, lack of preparation would result in severe consequences.

Many people downplay the effects of a wild card. Sometimes, if you propose one of these scenarios out of context, people will think you are overreacting—crazy, ranting, Chicken Little. Yet, wild-card scenarios happen all the time, especially in response to major events. Imagine yourself in the 1980s trying to forecast geopolitics or global business in the 1990s without considering the possibility, however slim, that the Soviet Union would just one day collapse. That's a wild card. Few people made plans based on a world in which the Soviets just called it quits.

THE IMPACT/PROBABILITY MATRIX IN ACTION: NEW CLINICAL TRIAL DISCLOSURE LAWS

The matrix tool was useful during a recent project on the future of pharmaceutical regulations. A scandal about pharmaceutical companies arose when it became known that data about the effects of Vioxx were obscured and that the manufacturer of Paxil hid studies about its effects on children.

The Impact/Probability Matrix was used to explore the questions:

○ How much disclosure will be mandated?

○ How will it change strategies at pharmaceutical companies?

This is how the scenarios played out:

○ *Low Probability, Low Impact—"False Alarm."* The crisis over the scandal goes away as the media tires of it.

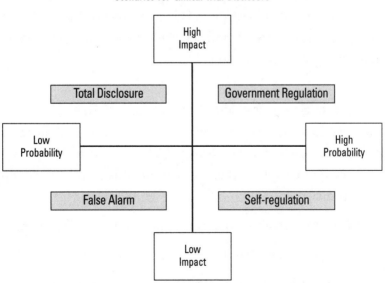

Scenarios for Clinical Trial Disclosure

FIGURE 6–2. Impact/probability matrix: clinical trial disclosure laws.

○ *High Probability, Low Impact—"Self-Regulation."* The government assumes that as long as pharmaceutical companies change their behavior, there is no need for additional legislation.

○ *High Probability, High Impact—"Government Regulation."* The government assumes pharmaceutical companies won't change *without* strong regulation, and new legislation forces greater transparency in clinical trials.

○ *Low Probability, High Impact—Total Disclosure.* The nightmare scenario, in which the public's trust in pharmaceutical companies is so shaken that the government demands all activities be made part of a public database. Companies scramble to learn how to compete in a world where everybody knows what they are doing years in advance.

The Impact/Probability Matrix is one way to arrange a number of scenarios without prejudicing any one of them. In this way, you can track trends and determine which might come true and determine how to respond.

You Do It: Scenarios About the Future of Beer

Now we have to take what we know to create scenarios that communicate the future of beer. Pick four of the trends we uncovered in Chapter 3 (here is a refresher list, but it's really up to your imagination).

○ China is becoming the world's biggest market for beer.

○ American beer brands are expanding overseas.

○ Aluminum is becoming a more popular packaging choice.

○ Americans are drinking more wine and spirits, but beer is falling in popularity, especially among younger consumers.

○ Craft brews are gaining in popularity, and regional pride is important.

Given these trends and others you may be tracking, combine these insights to show exactly what the beer industry of the future could look like. Start with the data and tell a story.

SCENARIO #1: MASS CUSTOMIZATION (OR, HOW YOU CAN GET YOUR OWN BEER)

The trends show that although mass beer consumption is falling, craft brews with local associations are doing better every year. The larger trend in manufacturing is mass customization, the application of flexible manufacturing techniques and information technology to provide each customer with an individual experience. Car companies are already letting customers design exactly the cars they want with a host of options. Couldn't beer do this, right down to the label? This scenario could show a company ordering its very own brand of craft-brewed beer, for not much more than mass-produced varieties.

SCENARIO #2: ACTIVE PACKAGING

We know that information technology such as RFID tags and small, inexpensive sensors could add more information-processing technology even to simple packages. This scenario could show how active packaging, the confluence of IT and materials science, could change how beer is delivered. The question is, What new services or improvements are now possible?

SCENARIO #3: BEER? WHO DRINKS THAT?

Ooh, a disruptive scenario in which (let us hang our heads) beer drinking is largely passé. The opposite of a normative scenario, and, for some of us, a nightmare scenario. In this scenario, you can use the trends we discovered to uncover a world filled with vodka, malt-alcohol-energy drinks, and this year's Beaujolais Villages, but, sadly, no Sam Adams.

> Frat guys, 2021: Dude, it was so weird. My frat brother John had his wacky uncle Russ in town, and he came to our Alpha Alpha October bash. Old dude, in his 40s, but still likes to party. He actu-ally brought an entire keg of beer to the party. Who was going to get through that? I think we all had one or two, but it doesn't mix well with vodka, so there was a ton left over. You know anybody who still drinks this stuff?

o   o   o

People like stories. If you want them to remember why the future is important, learn to tell stories, because once you discover how your organization will change in years to come, you'll need to communicate it to your colleagues. It isn't easy, but in Chapter 7, we'll look at the best practices available.

CHECKLIST: Scenarios

✔ Remember that stories are "stickier" than lists. Implications are useful to understand what trends mean, but if you want people to remember why they should care, tell them a story.

✔ Scenarios are really about people. Step into the shoes of the person in your scenario. If you are writing about the automotive industry, imagine someone fixing the car of 2021. What tools does he need? Is there still a role for mechanics, or are fuel-cell vehicles so simple you can fix them with a wrench and screwdriver?

✔ Scenarios should follow the trends, forecasts, and implications you discovered throughout your study. For example, take four trends and make sure they are reflected in each scenario. This way, scenarios are not based on your creative-writing ability; they reflect rigorously collected trend data and are thus more reliable.

✔ Name your scenarios, such as "Frat Party of the Future," or "Grandma Goes to the Dentist 2025." This is a useful way to make your scenarios more memorable.

WHAT YOU CAN DO TODAY

1. You haven't yet conducted your in-depth study of trends and forecasts? (I hope you're thinking about doing so!) Surely there is at least one development you are nervous about: global warming, aging populations, consumers in greater debt. For every issue that troubles you, try the Impact/Probability Matrix. On a sheet of paper draw four quadrants and put a potential scenario in each: Flash in the Pan, Business as Usual, The Brewing Storm, and Wild Card. Consider every issue going a total of four ways and get used to thinking in terms of *alternative futures*.

2. Have you got more in-depth scenarios built around your own research? Bravo! Looking for ways to communicate to others? See Chapter 7 for hints on some.

CHAPTER SEVEN

communicating the future

even to the skeptical

Y ou now have a lot of information to share with your colleagues about what is coming next. Can you believe it? You now know what is going to drive the future of the beer industry. If you have been reading this book with your own job or company in mind, you probably know about the future of what you do, too. Maybe you work for the post office and see a new world of postal communications. You may have uncovered different scenarios for the future of the hospital in which you work. Perhaps you are a farmer who has had enough of the breakneck change of the past decade and want a look ahead to see if you should continue growing hops or barley for beer.

I have some bad news, however. While you were training your mental muscles in the art of futuring, your colleagues, other members of the school board, other people you know, perhaps even your spouse didn't go on this trip with you. They might not accept the principle that a nonprofessional can have a sharper view of the future just by using tools that are accessible to anybody. They might be unwilling to hear what the future looks like, and, even if they are, they might not perceive that they have the time to do anything about it. They might even say something like, "Are you kidding? Are we wasting money studying the future? This company is so screwed up; we need to fix it today! Besides everybody knows you can't know what's going to happen next, so there's no point in trying. We really must focus on cost cutting. Things are really competitive out there!"

If you run your own business, great. You get to make the decisions about what happens next. If you are an entrepreneur, it's pretty straightforward. Maybe you read about the effect the retirement of the Baby Boomers will have and decided to start a travel agency dedicated to older people who have the time and money to travel extensively. Working by yourself, you can be more nimble with these decisions than big corporations are. Perhaps you run a video store and you see that in a few years you'll be able to e-mail entire DVDs in five seconds. You can sell the business and get out. Strategic analysis of the future can produce action quickly when you don't have to get decisions through a committee.

If, however, you work with employees, peers, or there are layers of management above you, you are faced with the question of how to lead change. Companies with 10,000 employees, for example, don't change overnight. (But then again, neither do companies employing 12 people.) One way or another, it's going to take real effort to turn the ship around.

Many people have had to face this dilemma. By studying the future, they gain important knowledge about what's coming next, including all the danger signals and interesting opportunities. Then, they actually have to go to work. They have to face the great majority of people who, naturally, may not see unexpected changes, people who haven't been studying the trends or exploring the possibilities. You need to explain the future to the bean counters and colleagues getting ready to retire who may be stuck in their ways.

But not to worry! Now you're a champion of the future, the one person in your organization who has the tools to see the future in a way that has been proved in hundreds of world-class organizations. You can learn from people in those organizations who communicated the future and won support for change.

Deciding When to Break the News

Luckily, the future is a topic that always fascinates people. They may be skeptical about your ability to see it, but there's nobody who isn't interested in what the future will bring. On the other hand, interesting people in what's next can be a matter of timing. In recent decades, the taste for futures work has come and gone. In the twentieth century, there were several periods in which the public hungered for news about the future. The Roaring Twenties, the Space Age 1950s, the Nuclear 1960s, and the pre-Millennium 1990s were times when people saw the world changing before their eyes and wanted to know more about how it might turn out. During such periods, it is easy to talk about the future, because individuals, decision makers, and media outlets thirst for the input of those who make serious work of looking at the future.

Then there are times when that enthusiasm diminishes. When times are tougher, people tend to be more defensive and focus on today. People's interest in the future certainly lost steam in the early 2000s, as the stock market crash, Enron, and September 11 made them more interested in securing what they already had—defense, petroleum, gold. Innovation became risky. Cynicism mounted; you heard more things like, "The rich get richer; the poor get poorer." Possibilities were harder to see. Now, as the world realizes that innovation will go on, the future is coming back. The time is right for you to lead others in your business or industry into looking ahead!

Deciding How to Break the News

You have a new mission: Talk to accountants about the future. All the information you gathered won't have its full effect if it just stays in your head. You have to be able to transmit that knowledge to others so they can think about their decisions with a sense of the future. The goal of studying the future is not simply to make forecasts and scenarios sound plausible at a cocktail party. The *real* goal is to be able to communicate what you have learned to the most shortsighted, specialized, and skeptical people in your organization. Buy in from all major sectors of the organization is essential if your group is going to change.

Let's say the small band of *futuristas* in your organization, or you all by yourself, launch a study of the future. You have to tell everybody the potential threats and opportunities. You hope that this previously undiscovered information will inspire the people around you to action. You know that your engineers should be working to design some new product. Maybe you'll merge with another company to brace for a strategic change that will leave only a couple of companies in your industry standing. It's time to get moving! How do you get the message heard?

If you work in a large organization, you have several tools available:

The Big Report. You can always gather your research into one giant report and make big, heavy copies for all of your colleagues, hoping they read the trends, forecasts, and implications. On the plus side, you'll have plenty of data to back up any conclusions. Writing everything down is good, especially if your colleagues require many details. On the minus side, most of your colleagues have enough to read all day, so they may not get through the volume of information you provided. Your report could become "credenzaware," a giant report in a binder that sits on a shelf unread.

Executive Summaries. Many organizations have had good success by taking the most important bits of the study and putting them into one PowerPoint presentation that is short and easy to read. This might include the 10 most important trends, major implications, and several potential scenarios of the future. These are nice because they are short and more likely to be read. Just make sure you have the Big Report ready and waiting; your more skeptical colleagues may want to see the data backing up the conclusions in your summary.

"Days in the Future." Many organizations, such as IBM and DuPont, find it useful to pull employees together for a day in the future. Based on the conclusions of your study of the future, companies will ask people to think about running their business in a world like the ones described in the scenarios. These simulations can last a few hours or several days, depending on how much material you want to cover. This practice makes people, even for a day, put themselves in the shoes of people living in the future. It's an exercise that transcends the written report and makes the conclusions feel more real.

Newsletters. Let's assume people have read the report, they have sent your conclusions on to their colleagues, and they attended the day in the future. How do you make sure they don't forget these insights? You have to remind people that the future is still out there. That which looked like a threat still needs to be tracked. People in the organization need to hear regular reports about the most important trends. One way to accomplish this is to publish a newsletter. It could be a regular e-mail with links to news stories, or it could be an actual newsletter, online or in printed form. The benefit of a newsletter is that it keeps people thinking about what's coming—the antidote to credenzaware.

A major soft drink company did this with great success by having its internal team of futurists publish a newsletter that was distributed companywide. This small, regular publication told the company's associates not just about the world of the future, but what the company would be doing differently as a result. The newsletters were distributed on a regular basis, covering new technologies for vending machines, customers of the future, sugar and associated agricultural trends, anything that could influence the company's core businesses. They also covered broader cultural topics, such as an interesting take on the future of holidays. The beverage giant wanted to know how people will celebrate the special days of the future and whether food and beverage would play a starring role in twenty-first-century celebrations. Its newsletter on the future was only a few pages per quarter, but the information was enough to keep employees apprised of the fact that they were part of an evolving organization.

Deciding How to Counter Attacks

Now that you have started spreading the message of the future, what should you do if skeptics start attacking the credibility of your work? The best futures work will meet some form of resistance. As I've said, you had better hope it meets resistance, or your work will not have challenged people enough to be of any use.

Occasionally, however, you have valuable insights, and people reject them wholesale. To make sure your colleagues hear what you have uncovered and can act upon it, your view of the future must be perceived as credible. After all, you are talking, with some authority, about things that haven't happened yet. It's one thing to speak when you have historical data to back up your conclusions. It's another when you are talking about things that haven't yet happened.

If you have followed the methodology thus far, you have a great advantage. Skepticism about your analysis can be overcome by presenting the hard data you uncovered and being transparent about the process you used. Some colleagues may initially reject the very notion of foresight; if so, remind them of the incisive words of Ian Pearson, British Telecom's famed futurist: "Blurry vision is better than none at all."[1]

What's more, you can win over the skeptics. Thanks to your research, the data is there. The methodology for arriving at new strategies is transparent. You can describe the tools that led to the implications and the scenarios you present. If someone disputes the validity, explain that futurism is employed by hundreds, if not thousands, of world-class institutions, in major corporations as well as government agencies.

At the end of the day, there is only one answer to people skeptical about strategic study of the future: We might not be completely accurate when we look at what is coming, but it sure is better than just plowing ahead in ignorance.

The Future Forever: Incorporating Futuring into How You Think

As much as I love being a futurist, I truly admire those who have to implement strategies for the future. After you close this book, you have to run schools, companies, government services, and your lives. That's the challenge of this process. Few people become full-time futurists, but anyone can learn to think like one. By learning how to follow trends and interpret them, you will change the way you read magazines, watch TV, make a five-year business plan, or invest.

Many people experience an awakening as soon as they begin this practice. It's as if somebody lifted a veil from their eyes, and suddenly they realize just how much is changing, from the mundane to the spectacular. Whether it is beer or nanotechnology, they realize the world is in a constant state of flux, which gives us an incredible opportunity to make things better. Yes, there is the possibility that we will make things worse, especially if we are thoughtless about how what we do changes the future.

I look out at the future and see more opportunity than ever. I have no idea whether we will use it for good or evil, for constructive means or destructive chaos. If humanity's past is any indication, then it will probably be a mix of both. One thing is clear—people are far more likely to make wise decisions about the future if they know more about it.

Consider the nuclear brinksmanship of the Cold War. Many people who are too young to remember or have forgotten about this conflict are therefore very nervous about terrorism and the uncertainty it has caused. What we should not overlook is the fact that for decades the United States and the former Soviet Union were ready on a moment's notice to destroy most of the cities on Earth.

One of the many reasons we did not create a nuclear winter is that we began using futures studies to predict instability. Herman Kahn, the father of scenario planning, worked for the Defense Department during the Cold War. He worked with leaders to consider several scenarios in which we had a nuclear exchange with the USSR. Most of these scenarios were bad. It was exploring the future and seeing how awful it could be that taught our leaders to step more carefully in the Cold War.

This type of scenario creation also illustrates one of the best reasons for a forecast to be inaccurate: People see a terrible future approaching and *change their behavior* to make something different happen.

The same is true of you and your journey into the future. By studying what's next, you don't have to be doomed to that future. You can change it. For example, you may see that your major products are about to become obsolete. The forecast says that your company will go bankrupt in six years. With this new knowledge, maybe you jump early to get into a new market, developing new products for new times. If you're a small business, maybe you realize now is a good time to sell the business and start a new career. In any event, you don't have to be resigned to following through on a bad future; you can control your own fate, but that is hard to do if you aren't paying attention.

In every part of business and government, the coming decades promise enormous changes. I hope you are as honored and excited as I am to lead in this interesting era. We have tremendous amounts of choice available to us. Let us then keep an eye on what's next to choose the best future possible.

CHECKLIST: Communications

✔ Remember, you learned a lot and most people did not go on the journey with you. Write for the most short-sighted people you can imagine.

✔ Lean on the data you collected from the experts to support your position.

✔ Any time you disseminate your insights about the future to colleagues, make sure you have the basic data to back it up. Don't talk about implications and scenarios unless you can provide written proof of all the trends that went into your conclusions.

✔ You will likely meet somebody who thinks that the whole idea of looking ahead is impossible. Remember, "Blurry vision is better than none."

✔ In the end, the study of the future isn't about being *right* about what the world of 2024 will look like. It's about seeing change and choosing the best future. We're not clairvoyant, but we are powerful enough to change our future.

WHAT YOU CAN DO TODAY

1. Be the champion for the future. Let your colleagues know that you are collecting strategic trends, and invite them in to interpret the data you uncover.

2. Start an e-mail list or small newsletter in which you periodically keep your colleagues updated on trends. It doesn't have to be a major publication; it might just be a list of Web links. Make sure that "the future" is a regular part of everybody's thinking, not just an exercise you do when it's time to do a five-year strategic plan.

PART 2

Drivers of the Future

YOU HAVE JUST learned how to study the future for whatever it is that you do. It's a time-tested methodology that produces valuable insight for leaders all over the world. Hopefully, by now you are hooked and want to make thinking about the future a part of your everyday life. Your next questions are probably: What will I be looking at? Just what is driving all that change? Where should I start? What can I do today to prepare?

You might be studying the future of anything, from nanotechnology to pharmaceutical sales forces, agriculture to semiconductors, schizophrenia medication to electronics in the car. When you do enough of these studies, you see a pattern. Every study is not entirely from scratch based on completely different trends. There are larger trends that affect us all, every industry, in different ways. Most things are being changed by the fabulous new capabilities in information technology. No matter what we do, we depend on scarce energy resources. And it's hard to look out 15 years and not wonder how the mass retirement of the Baby Boomers is going to change things.

So to help you on your journey, here is something more than just the methodology of how to study the future. The following chapters are about the major drivers of the future, those areas that need exploration in every study. In studies of the future, we always come back to aging populations, energy, environmental sustainability, IT, health care, biotechnology, and the proliferation of media. The following chapters just scratch the surface of the topics and by no means are intended to be complete explorations of the subjects. Instead, they are a collection of what constantly comes up in studies of the future, so whether you are a giant corporation or a small business, these are all forces that will change you.

Nor are these the only trends you'll need to study. Business trends such as outsourcing and globalization, political trends, consumer behavior—they all could be vital to your study of the future. But the following topics are poised to make some of the biggest impact for the broadest number of people.

Moreover, since each topic here pertains to you in some way, there are proactive steps you can take today to prepare for these changes. Included here are some suggestions about what most organizations will need to do. Discuss them with your colleagues to explore how these implications will apply to you specifically.

CHAPTER EIGHT

aging

preparing for a
new grey world

ll over the world, people will have the thermo-stat up to 80. The dinner rush at restaurants will start at 4:30 in the afternoon. Millions will be driving around slowly with their turn signals on for miles. Shuffleboard will replace soccer and basketball as the world's favorite sports.

That's right—the most powerful force in the world over the next 20 years will be legions of old people, the largest generation of retirees in history. As they say in the fashion world, "Grey will be the new black."

Industrialized countries are bracing themselves for the grey invasion. People often ask futurists to tell them the one thing that will change in the future. For many, the first thing that leaps to mind is aging populations. Because of the high number of births in the post-WWII era and advances in health care, the world's largest generation will also live longer than any other in history.

The world has never experienced as many millions of old people as it will in the next few decades. In the next 30 years, America, Europe, Japan, and China will be full of pensioners. America alone is expecting its retired population to increase from 35 million people to over 70 million, specifically when the Baby Boom population retires around 2015. Europe, Japan, and China are expecting similar situations, exacerbated by low fertility rates.

The implications here are staggering. On the one hand, this represents an enormous market for new products, and perhaps a new and overwhelming demand for government services, but the stress so many old people put on an economy could destabilize it. The young will each have several old people to support in terms of taxes and the cost of social programs. This is upside down. When our social safety nets were created in the mid–twentieth century, old people died at a faster rate than young people did, so the proportion reversed. Our social systems were not designed to care for retired people for decades on end. In America, especially, the Baby Boomers will be in an unprecedented position. They represent an enormously powerful voting bloc, but they will no longer be the major wage earners and contributors to productivity.

The potential stress on the economy and social fabric of a nation resulting from millions of senior citizens would not have such a negative impact if there were an equal number of young people to support that generation, pay for government social services, and take their place in the workforce. However, because the Baby Boom truly was a larger-than-average generation in many countries, there will not be a similarly sized generation of young people to support this retirement. Many countries are bracing themselves for what is ahead.

Italy, for example, has the greatest percentage of elderly people and the lowest birthrate in the world—1.3 babies per couple.[1] Given this combination, the country has a daunting task ahead of it. The home of pasta, Lamborghinis, and fancy shoes is unquestionably a welfare state, and its laws allow some workers to retire in their *forties*. Naturally, Italians expect paid retirements. Given today's medical technology, the country expects that many people will live three, four, and five decades past the time they exit the workforce. Somebody has to work in order to pay for those retirement benefits, and the Italian government is having a tough time figuring out whom that will be. Moreover, Italian villages will see the worst of this crisis, because young people are fleeing the provinces for Rome and Milan.

Italy will need people to drive its economy, continue its culture, and care for its ballooning population of seniors. What can it do? This dire demographic situation may soon call for desperate measures. Immigration from North Africa and Eastern Europe is already causing unrest among European countries, especially since the riots in France and the Netherlands. Italians might have to tap into a resource it has long forgotten. This is just one scenario, but I submit that Italy could begin soliciting Italian immigrants from New Jersey and Long Island to make up for a lack of native Italians back home.

Crazy? Perhaps, but the cost of living in the New York metropolitan area is outrageous, and the pace doesn't suit everyone. Italy might be excited to offer citizenship to the Mazzariello and Del Veneri and Vericchio families it lost years ago. American immigrants going the *other direction* could find cheap land and easy job opportunities in the sunny villages where their grandparents lived. Italians could revitalize their country, and Italian-Americans could avoid facing the problem of million-dollar condos in Manhattan. Sunny villas in Campania and Puglia are going for less than half of what homes cost in New Jersey, and restoring older buildings is even cheaper. I might be crazy, but it could be a win-win.

For that matter, Japan is facing the same problem as Italy. The Land of the Rising Sun has a burgeoning cohort of old people and a birthrate of less than 1.5 babies per couple. Unlike the United States (or possibly, if you follow my scenario, Italy), Japan cannot rely on immigration to bring new blood into the country. Japan has no history of accepting new ethnic groups into Japanese culture. Whereas the United States can allow Latinos to emigrate to the country in the hope of becoming naturalized American citizens, Japan's immigration laws do not afford citizenship as readily. Still, Japan is facing the same shortage of young people that it will need to provide vitality to the economy and to support its elderly. As a result, in the future the Japanese may not be able to be as ethnically exclusive in granting permanent citizenship. They may need to be much more welcoming to Filipinos and Koreans just to keep from going bankrupt.

Future Boom—The Me Generation Changes the Nature of Retirement

Not only will this be the largest group of older people ever; it will be different from elderly groups of the past. From now on, elderly people will be nearly as healthy, active, and connected as their younger counterparts. They will travel. They will play sports. They will keep working if they so desire. They will be richer than any group of elderly before them, and they will spend that money on entertainment, among other things. In addition, they will be using the most expensive health care system in history.

Many countries are preparing for aging populations, but America is preparing for something even more—the Baby Boom retirement. Perhaps no generation in history has had as much influence as the massive group born after the Second World War. It has captured the attention of America at every stage of life. In the 1950s, it was time for rock 'n' roll. In the 1960s, suddenly you could not trust anyone over 30—the "kids were all right"—and as soon as the pill came on the scene, it was time for a sexual revolution. In the 1970s, unready to launch into full adulthood, America entered the Me Decade and the Disco Era. That was until it was time to buy houses and settle down in the 1980s, when America embraced Reagan conservatism, the movie *Wall Street*, and the idea that "greed is good." In the 1990s, suddenly, life began at *forty*. Now, it's *fabulous at fifty*, and you can't get away from The Beatles and The Doors on the radio.

Clearly, the Boomers are *not* the "Silent Generation." At every stage, they transfix America with what they are going through. Retirement will be no different. These are people who get what they want.

For example, the term *in loco parentis* means "in place of parent," in Latin. It described the system that pertained at American universities. In practice, it meant the college could dictate the social as well as the educational aspects of its students' lives—even what time they were going to go to bed. This system lasted for decades, centuries even—until the Boomers arrived at college.

In the 1960s, colleges were giving 20-year-olds a "bedtime" when, at the same moment, the government was shipping their peers off to die in Viet Nam. Boomers, noting they were old enough to take a bullet and die in a rice paddy but not allowed to decide when to go to bed, protested, and they had the sheer numbers to enforce their will. The universities capitulated, and *in loco parentis* was no more. From that moment on, young people could count on having more personal freedom when they went to college. Boomers changed America everywhere they went.

Now, do we really expect these same people to slip quietly into retirement, putting up with neglect, marginalization, and an expensive, dilapidated health care system? Do we expect them to consign themselves to rocking chairs and meager fixed incomes? Unlikely. Expect the Boomers to demand better service from health care. They'll demand employment opportunities out of sheer boredom. Their lives will focus on continual growth, enrichment, and opportunities. Don't expect Boomers to let the rest of the country just forget about them. They sure haven't in the past, and now, in the United States at least, they have the financial resources and free time to make a big noise in America.

The HR Implosion: The Skilled-Labor Gap

In addition to straining health care resources, aging populations affect society in other ways. Many companies, including the federal government, are facing the possibility that about half of their workforce is about to retire. Fifty percent of the U.S. civil service is eligible to retire at any time. Companies such as Lockheed Martin have commented that they are getting ready to lose large numbers of their engineers to retirement. Naturally, due to demographics, the younger generation simply isn't as big, and the U.S. as a country did not concentrate its resources on encouraging the next generation to become engineers. Many employers are wondering how they are going to replace the millions of skilled workers getting ready to leave the workforce.

Combine this with another trend: Increasing competition and technological progress is leading to greater specialization among more companies. So although there will be millions of jobs opening, companies won't be looking for just another warm body they may not even be able to train. Companies will be losing salespeople, engineers, product designers, and other skilled employees who grew with their industries. When they leave, many companies want to replace them with another skilled worker already familiar with the industry and do not want to do the training. They want employees ready to work, "right out of the box."

For example, during the worst of the recession of 2002, an engineer at IBM once told me, "Sure we're hiring at IBM, but we're looking for engineers who are already familiar with the manufacture of integrated circuits. We don't even want regular electrical engineers. The job has been open for three years, and it will probably be open even longer."

The faster industries change, the less willing companies are to train. They want *pharmaceutical* salespeople, people who write *bank-networking* software, and people who know human resources for the *fashion apparel* industry. Experience is nice, but specialization sells.

If you haven't seen this trend developing, just ask recent college graduates. They sure know. Those kids are the ones lining up to add an extra $50,000 in debt in order to get a master's degree, because companies want pretrained, ready-to-go young workers who already have a master's in *information technology* business management or *telecommunications* law. A good education and ambition are not always enough to land a job in today's marketplace.

Of course, in the next 10 years, employers may not be able to be so choosy when half the skilled workforce retires. They might actually have to train people and entice them to stay, a little bit like the old days.

If they don't want to replace their retired workforce with capable but untrained young people, there are many firms in Bangalore or Mumbai with skilled workers waiting to pick up the slack in case Western companies decide to outsource the entire thing to them.

Filling the Gap: The Retired Part-Timer to the Rescue

On the other hand, let's not count the retired workforce out just yet. A few countertrends may mitigate the damage of all that talent drain. Maintaining one's health is a major focus for retired people, not to mention making a little more money to shore up social security and retirement accounts.

Even though a lifetime of work is preparing seniors for a long healthy retirement, the only way to stay healthy is *not to retire!* New studies show that complete retirement, the kind where you sit in a rocking chair, is the enemy of health. Preliminary results of a U.S. National Bureau of Economic Research working paper (March 2006) entitled "The Effects of Retirement on Physical and Mental Health Outcomes" indicate that complete retirement leads to a 23 to 29 percent increase in difficulties associated with mobility and daily activities, an 8 percent increase in illness, and an 11 percent decline in mental health.[2] The National Institute on Alcohol Abuse and Alcoholism says that drinking increases markedly among the fully retired. Some nursing homes report a drinking problem among 49 percent of full-time residents.[3] Experts assume that lack of purpose leads to a sedentary lifestyle and depression.

There is good news for those who miss the workforce! Because fewer jobs today require backbreaking physical labor or inhaling coal dust all day, there is rarely a physical reason most people must retire at age 65. Many lucrative jobs will be well within the physical abilities of retirees. Most professors, lawyers, office workers, and even tradespeople have the physical capacity to remain in the workplace if they choose to do so. This could increase the number of consultants, outsourced, and part-time workforce considerably and help fill the expertise gap that might otherwise rock businesses around the world.

Retirees will demand part-time work, new careers, and different ways to contribute to society, which is good, because our social programs were not designed for the life expectancies of people today. Merrill Lynch's recent "New Retirement Survey" shows that Boomers currently reject the idea of full-time leisure or full-time work when thinking about retirement. They will instead choose cyclic periods of work and leisure—six months working down at the shop or consulting, followed by six months doing other things like travel, hobbies, and volunteer work.[4]

Real estate agents already see this trend taking shape. One agent in the rural Eastern Shore of Maryland reports that whereas he normally would be selling second homes to retired people from Washington, D.C., there is an increasing demand for houses with ample home offices. Retiring Boomers, it seems, are stepping down from their careers in stages, not simply quitting and completely replacing one lifestyle with another. Information workers, in particular, find that their expertise is in demand and that they can continue their careers for years in a reduced capacity if that's what they desire. This could be good news for employers, who can have continued access to all the skills of these workers and make the transition to a new workforce in stages.

New Products to Keep Older People Independent and Happy

Tomorrow's retirees are looking at a healthier, more active life. Still, there are certain realities. As people age, they will eventually face a variety of physical and medical problems. Knees get creaky. Eyesight goes bad. That doesn't mean that older people are going to accept boredom and poor health—if they can help it. Below are some of the goods and services this greying society will need to keep it happy and functioning.

HOUSEWARES

Companies will design a wide range of everyday products for those with arthritic hands and blurrier eyesight. It is already happening. OXO brand kitchen tools—the ones with nice fat handles—have the elderly in mind. Imagine that kind of design applied to myriad other products. Redesigning the world so it is more readily accessible to older people will not only result in happier, more independent older people; it will save millions if not billions in the cost of assisted living.

There will be tremendous business opportunities arising from this trend. As the Baby Boomers age, for example, homes will have to adapt to the needs of older people who may not have children living nearby to help with the tasks of day-to-day living. Designers will need to make stoves, microwaves, can openers, and bathrooms useful to the older person. "Smart homes" that combine information technology and safer designs, can track people's movements, help prevent injury, and warn caregivers if an accident has occurred could fill many of these needs. Advances in sensor technology and IT will make a smart house of the future more possible, especially as the devices become increasingly interoperable. The home network of the not-too-distant future could call for an ambulance in the event of a fall or serious health problem.

TRANSPORTATION

Getting around independently enhances people's quality of life as they age. The Japanese, recognizing that their population is aging, have quantified this in an academic study. According to the Japan Aging Resource Center, the society of the future must allow older people to get around on their own. However, as people age their reflexes slow and their eyesight may be poor, and therefore many stop driving—or remain on the roads, creating the possibility of accidents, which are dangerous for them and others. Cars will become onerous for the retiree and dangerous for society. Still, people will demand independence later in life. The need for improved automotive technology designed with the elderly in mind, as well as alternative forms of transportation, is apparent.

There will be a market for vehicles that help aging people continue to drive—sensors to warn of danger ahead, perhaps even a heads-up display that would magnify the road and enhance vision and mitigate hearing loss. Undergraduate engineering students at Johns Hopkins University have designed a harness that will help protect those with brittle bones in the event of a car crash. The General Motors mobility team just invented the "Sit-N-Lift," which helps elderly and disabled people get in and out of automobiles easily and comfortably. For easier transportation within cities, elderly people may need something besides the potentially dangerous automobile. Toyota has just released a robotic city walker that will transport people with low mobility comfortably and quickly. It's strange to think about robot-like armies of elderly people walking around our cities, but shouldn't every book about the future talk about at least one futuristic gadget?

ENTERTAINMENT

Very few people are talking about the immense needs for entertainment that an aging population will have. The retirees of 2020 are members of today's fast-paced environment; they are accustomed to fast-paced information and active lifestyles.

Especially while they are still relatively young, they will want an active retirement, and, because families are more geographically dispersed than ever before, they will be traveling more.

The retirement of the Baby Boomers will lead to an increase in what is currently called "accessible tourism." This branch of the tourism industry currently caters to handicapped and elderly clients who wish to enjoy travel while avoiding the obstacles they might encounter at destinations not designed for those with limited mobility.[5]

Because this generation of retirees will have more leisure time than they had when working full-time, there will be a tremendous increase in the need for services that keep them entertained and engaged. Up to half of Boomers are worried about serious illness at some time in their future, meaning, according to the Merrill Lynch survey, health clubs that promise physical activity will be popular. Music, movies, theater, and home entertainment will be important as well.

SEX

Senior-citizen sex is not something you read about every day, but in a novel turn of events the increased number of healthy older people is bringing to light a formerly little-discussed subject—sex later in life. If the media was your only source of information, you would think that sex is the dominion only of the young—unless you count Jack Nicholson and Michael Douglas, who always seem to fall in love with younger actresses both on screen and off—and you would be wrong. Studies show that there is no significant loss of sexual desire or sexual activity in the silver years, which, based on statistics, would mean that sex is actually the dominion of the old!

In 1989, Judy Bretschneider and Norma McCoy conducted a study of 200 nursing-home residents with a median age of 86 (respondents were between the ages of 81 and 101!) to examine their sexual habits. The vast majority of these seniors, both men and women, thought about sex regularly. A majority engaged in some sort of physical intimacy, and 66 percent of the men claimed to be engaged in regular intercourse. The study showed that people tend to have sex into advanced age unless obesity or illness stunts their bodies, possibly precluding sexual activity at any age. Furthermore, the test group of the Bretschneider-McCoy study was raised in an era that did not nearly have the sexually positive attitudes of those who came of age just after World War II.[6] One can only assume that the Baby Boomers, with their more-open attitudes toward healthy sex, will enjoy it for at least as long as seniors today. Just think—if medical technology extends the normal life span into the nineties or hundreds, then the average person could be sexually active for 80 years.

This might not be the first thing people consider when looking at the Boomer retirement, but because the majority of consumer products are sold to enhance our status and attractiveness to the opposite sex, there will be many business opportunities.

HOUSING

Real estate will change dramatically when this mass retirement occurs. The places today's retirees congregate are becoming full and expensive. This can be a perfect opportunity for other communities that can accommodate retirees—places able to provide or build their infrastructure to balance peace and quiet with good roads to get people to and from small cities, among others.

The retirement of the Boomers could be the force that makes many cities function more as communities. Boomers will want a pedestrian-centered community atmosphere for safety and ease of access. Cities will need to redesign their centers with older residents in mind. Cities surrounded by far-flung suburbs will not be practical.

In addition, some retirees may choose to live in other countries. The economic stresses and rising costs in the United States could force retirees on fixed incomes to seek retirement in other countries. Mexico and the Philippines might attempt to boost local economies by offering improved standards of living in exchange for an influx of pensioners from rich nations.

Regardless of location, there are three types of living arrangements a greying population will influence:

1. *Assisted Living.* There will be an undeniable explosion in the need for assisted-living communities. As longevity increases, the number of people in need of some form of help will necessarily increase.

2. *Nursing-Home Living.* Diseases of the body and mind, such as Alzheimer's, which costs significantly more to treat than any other disease and is expected to affect twice as many people in the next 20 years, will require more care than assisted living can provide.

3. *Hospice and Other End-of-Life Care.* Think of the amount of time and energy we will be spending in the 2020s and 2030s burying and remembering people. As the Boomers die, the need for mortuary services and related services will increase sharply. The National Funeral Directors Association, comfortingly, reports that there is an increase in the overall professionalization of the funeral industry.[7] Governments are requiring higher standards of practice and mortuary professionals are receiving additional education before receiving certification to

operate a funeral business. Another trend is the increase in the additional services that funeral homes provide to families, particularly remembrance services and support groups.

Impact of the Coming Transfer of Wealth

We are about to witness the largest transfer of wealth in history. As the Silver Generation dies, leaving its wealth to the Baby Boom generation, America's largest, most prosperous generation will leave its wealth to Generation X. In the United States, philanthropic organizations are expecting $18 trillion to transfer from Boomers to Gen X. Note the contrast here. Society will be struggling to support members of the Boom generation in their winter years, but ultimately this will give way to transfers of wealth decades from now when they are gone.

CHARITABLE GIVING

Even as the economy has slowed, charitable giving in the U.S. has increased. There are more ways and more causes and organizations than ever to give money to. According to Changing Our World, Inc., a group that specializes in consulting to philanthropic organizations, there were 15,000 nonprofit organizations in the United States in 1940; today there are more than 700,000![8] One of the big "problems" nonprofits anticipate is what might happen if they suddenly have too much money. There are managerial problems that could arise when nonprofits suddenly have to grow because of all the money pouring in. These are the best kinds of problems, but still, the philanthropic community is preparing for a shock.

Dr. Susan Raymond, an expert in philanthropy, forecasts that if the influx of money creates as many jobs as it has in the past, the effect will be massive.[9] Even conservative estimates show that nonprofits could have as many as 21 million employees and

18 million volunteers. That's the population of Texas and California all working to improve society.

GEN X

The world's youths should feel grateful if they receive a portion of their parents' estates—older generations, including the Boomers, appear to be the last to have a robust savings rate. McKinsey & Company's most recent report on capital markets shows that although countries like Italy and Japan typically have had high savings rates, a sign of economic well-being, the smaller, younger generations don't save nearly as much.[10] Thus, young Italians and Japanese will already have the burden of taking care of huge phalanxes of senior citizens, and they won't have as much in savings for themselves when they reach retirement.

Young people of the industrialized world should get a piggy bank! Though some of you may inherit money, you will not benefit from the pensions and social networks of past generations. You may need the wealth the Boom generation will pass on to you to pay for things like your own health care and assisted-living expenses.

YOUTH IN THE MIDDLE EAST AND AFRICA

While the population of industrialized nations is aging, war and the AIDS epidemic will create the opposite phenomenon in other regions of the world. Africa and the Middle East will be full of younger people. According to the Brookings Institution, youths under the age of 24 currently make up 50 to 65 percent of the population of the Middle East.[11] There are already weak social services and few jobs waiting for these young people. Based on the demographics, this trend will not subside for decades, meaning the situation may only get worse. It remains to be seen whether Middle Eastern and African nations can harness this vitality or if a lack of opportunity for the young will further strain society.

CHECKLIST: Driving the Future of Aging

✔ There are an unprecedented number of aging people throughout the industrialized countries, and there are not enough young people to support them.

✔ Companies and government agencies are about to lose expertise and skills as this generation retires.

✔ The grey revolution will generate demand for new products and services that entertain, transport, feed, and care for the elderly.

✔ There will be an increased focus on end-of-life care.

✔ Baby Boomers are poised to receive the biggest transfer of wealth in history.

✔ At the same time, countries in the Middle East and Africa could struggle to find opportunities for their relatively large populations of young people.

IMPLICATIONS: Aging Populations

1. *You can't go wrong investing in keeping older people mobile, nourished, entertained, and connected to society.* Not only might it be a good business to be in; it will help society in ways big and small. Think about new services for this new generation of active retirees, but also on how to optimize what you already do for this newly important demographic.

2. *Think of how important child care is to your workforce; "elder care" will be even bigger than that.* Prepare for the future when your employees will require flexible schedules to help care for older family members who can no longer be left alone during the day. You may even need to give them an "elder care" center on site so they can meet family needs and work obligations at the same time. Remember, kids are in school once they reach age 5. Infirm elderly folks can need help for decades!

3. *You need to plan to keep valuable knowledge in your business.* Many businesses are knowledge driven, dependent on R&D, manufacturing know-how, and specialized knowledge. With so many experienced workers getting ready to retire, how will you make sure that the business can continue without that hard-earned knowledge? Will you write it down? Hire retirees to consult part-time? Expect new workers to have several degrees and already understand the industry? This is going to be a bigger challenge than most organizations realize. Get ahead of the curve, or you risk losing valuable knowledge.

4. *Prepare for the scarce commodity of talented young workers.* The sheer noise generated by the Boomer generation has often obscured the obvious fact that Generation X isn't as big. Just as industries become far more specialized to remain competitive, the overall pool of applicants is shrinking. Get ready to cultivate young talent now or face the rush to hire good candidates from Generations X and Y when the crunch is on.

CHAPTER NINE

information technology

falling in price, increasing in power

Picture in your mind what "information technology" looks like. You can see it now, stacks of giant IBM blade servers powering some critical application, or maybe a sleek laptop allowing you to work in a coffee shop. It's expensive. It breaks down often, requiring someone with superior technical ability to come fix it. The person shows up, mutters something about "corrupted disk sectors," and informs you that your last year of e-mails is now gone.

We use IT for everything; it is so central to our lives that many of us hyperventilate when we can't access our e-mail and documents. We use information technology to communicate, play games, make music, land airplanes, balance spreadsheets, design automobile parts, just about everything. For people today, IT is big, clunky, power hungry, hard to maintain, and very important.

In the future, you can expect more from IT. Information technology will become even smaller and lighter—but, more important, it will be easier to maintain and so cheap that everyday devices—even things like soda bottles and T-shirts—will integrate it. Devices will talk among themselves and even diagnose and fix most of their own problems. Instead of demanding babysitting from its users, IT will do its job of computation and shut up, letting humans do *their* work. For that matter, people may never hear the words "information technology." Most consumers will assume that modern technology can capture, sense, and process data, and then communicate it, wirelessly, and without much technical skill on the part of the user. IT will go beyond just being a "normal part of life" and become nearly invisible.

The Amazing, Disappearing Computer

One single trend is making the computer smaller and cheaper. For the last 40 years, computer processing and memory has declined in price while it increased in power. In fact, this trend has a name: Moore's Law. Intoned constantly in futures research, it was a forecast issued in 1965 that predicted transistor density would double every 18 months while price remained at parity. The law was named after Gordon Moore, former CEO of Intel, and for over 30 years his forecast has dominated the IT industry's expectations about computer-chip power and size.

As we all know, the computer keeps shrinking while doing increasingly more clever things. Fifty years ago, this meant fitting a computer in a single room. Later, it meant tucking it into the moon lander. Soon after, they came into our living rooms, then our cars, watches, Bluetooth headsets, toasters, and antilock brakes. In the next few years, the goal is to put sensing and processing power virtually anywhere.

How much processing power can we expect from IT in 10 years? For some perspective, I wrote and stored this book on a computer with a 120-gigabyte Western Digital hard drive. Cost: $200. Back in 1980, a company called North Star offered a state-of-the-art hard drive that featured 18 megabytes. Cost: $4,199. To put it another way, 26 years ago, my hard drive would have cost almost $28 million *if* it could have been made.

So what's next? Experts in IT assume that Moore's Law is going to remain true for at least the next 10 years. According to Marshall Brain, author of *How Stuff Works,* based on past trends of processor and memory development as tracked in *PC Magazine,* the top-of-the-line home computer of 2015 will likely feature:

○ A 1,000-GHz processor

○ Two thousand gigabytes of RAM

○ Two million gigs of hard-drive space

○ A video card with enough power to simulate human vision[1]

Moreover, we will be able to display information almost anywhere. Companies such as Boston's E Ink are developing small, low-power, flexible displays—a computer screen with all the properties of construction paper.

As far as connectivity goes, most cities are installing wireless infrastructure that will allow a world of data to flow through walls anywhere. More devices are able to communicate with each other and set up networks automatically. The business model of charging for access is temporary at best. Wireless Internet access will be like public toilets—we don't charge users for the water and maintenance; it is just part of a functioning city.

Computers of the future will increase significantly in power, work wirelessly, establish networks easily, and display their data in a variety of ways. We will all have enough data processing and memory to keep a video of every event in our entire lives. Or perhaps store a library of every movie ever made or record every phone call you ever make. Or design your own jet. The only limit on this power will be your imagination.

Computers You Don't Have to Babysit: The Next IT Revolution

As powerful as tomorrow's computers will be, this is not where the true revolution in computing lies. The future is not in smart, but in *dumb*. Well, not actually dumb, but IT that is small, cheap, and requires little power and less maintenance is the real future of IT. The race is on for cheap, disposable computers—devices that will put the power of information in places it can't yet go.

Supercomputers are here, if you stick enough expensive, hard-to-maintain, power-hungry computers together. The real killer apps of tomorrow, underserved by today's clunky machines, are the many tasks that require collecting a little data, computing it, and transmitting it.

Pharmaceuticals are a good example. The black market for prescription drugs is so great that many packages mysteriously walk off the truck. Think of the risk in shipping addictive opiate painkillers like OxyContin and Percoset—these pain medications essentially are pure versions of oral heroin. Trucking them is practically an invitation to hijacking, given the street value of the drugs. OxyContin needs packaging that might actually broadcast a message that says, in effect, "Hi, I'm a controlled substance. I was packaged in New Jersey. I should be taken off the truck in Florida. If I'm taken off the truck somewhere else, call the authorities!"

Enter Cypak AB, a Swedish company that released a disposable paperboard computer in 2004 that featured 32 kilobytes of secure memory. Using radio-frequency ID (RFID) technology, the disposable computer is perfect for pharmaceutical packaging, and in turn keeping tighter control of drugs so people do not steal them and sell them on the black market. When the computer is no longer needed, it can be safely discarded. More shippers today are using these technologies to create an added layer of security—without cheap disposable devices, it would simply be too expensive to pull off. All this is made possible by IT you do not have to babysit.

This packaging technology, made possible by inexpensive data processing, could serve other industries. We have already transitioned to self-checkout in some grocery stores, where shoppers scan their own groceries. With RFID falling in price, it will be possible to have fully automated checkout, where all your packages "talk" to the checkout computer at the same time. You fill your cart, push it through the checkout aisle, and pay. You bag it yourself. A major time saver and cost cutter, made possible by inexpensive IT.

There are endless applications for cheap, disposable IT. As we try to understand the environment, a proliferation of sensors measuring water and air quality will tell us how to avoid pollution. Installing sensors everywhere is far too expensive today, but when the price drops sufficiently, there are many things they can do.

One of my favorite examples of this is in agriculture. No, I don't mean we attach a computer chip to every potato to measure freshness, although if they can make a computer circuit out of butter and garlic that melts in a sauté pan, that might be interesting.

I mean that there is a need to reduce the use of pesticide. Pests ruin crops, but use too much pesticide, and it pollutes the groundwater. Often, farmers spray pesticide everywhere, no matter where the bugs are. This is wasteful.

Researchers came up with an unusual solution. They trained a dog to run through the field and to stop wherever the bugs were. Then, researchers put a global positioning system tracking device in the dog's collar. Satellites measured where the dog ran on the field, and that's where the farmers sprayed. Instead of wasting pesticide by using it everywhere, cheap IT and a well-trained dog cut pesticide use by 90 percent. No stacks of blade servers required.

The Big-Brother Generation of IT

Other applications will challenge our desire for privacy. For better or for worse, small video and audio devices will allow law enforcement and the military to surveil an exponentially larger number of places. With shrinking wireless video cameras and "micro air vehicles" the size of birds, we will be able to have a video camera in every corner of the city. Torrents of data about the whereabouts of all citizens will be available as cell phones gather GPS data on their users. We have only begun the civic discussion of how public authorities should behave when suddenly faced with extremely powerful information about the behavior of free people.

The Democratization of IT

Until very recently, IT has been something that required some form of training—either on the job or by taking special courses. Note that people still mention the ability to use Microsoft Office applications as a "skill" on résumés. The use of IT once represented modern business savoir faire.

Cheaper, lighter, and more robust IT will mean that people in developing economies will finally be able to use IT without special training, thus enabling them to take part in the global marketplace. For example, the Internet relies on some sophisticated knowledge among network engineers just to keep it going. Imagine trying to run an ISP in Afghanistan, Haiti, or Sudan in the past 10 years. How do you operate a server farm in a place where electricity is intermittent and the cost of air-conditioning is astronomical? On the user end, a typical PC might have cost several times the average person's annual salary. The telephone system would have been far too primitive to support Internet connectivity. In short, the past generation of IT was ill suited to such an environment, but small, inexpensive wireless devices that form networks automatically are perfect to connect people in far-off places.

That is the promise of tomorrow's IT, and it will give people who currently live in isolation a way to connect to economic, cultural, and educational opportunities that would have been otherwise impossible. Companies are designing a $100 laptop for use in developing economies. What happens when that price hits $10?

Not every business has to have its own computers connected by a local area network to be effective. India has been installing kiosks all over agricultural states. The kiosks electronically dispense information about crop conditions and fertilizer prices.[2] Today, these kiosks are nothing more than a PC and a wireless link to the Internet. They even allow farmers to bid their crops out on electronic markets such as e-Choupal. It would be unreasonable for poor Indian farmers to own their own computers at today's prices, so the village shares information technology. This simple access to data is lifting the standard of living for Indian farmers. Imagine what it might do when the technology is even cheaper and more robust so everyone can have his or her own computer.

People everywhere want access to information about the world they live in. As IT becomes more accessible, people in poverty and isolation will be able to connect with the rest of us. They will be able to improve their industries—whether its subsistence farming, textiles, or selling local arts and crafts—in ways that were previously impossible due to cultural and economic barriers. IT will go from being an elite technology, available only in industrialized countries, to being more egalitarian.

The Next Internet—People Powered

We may one day look at the past 10 years of the Internet as the time when we worked out the kinks and had many expensive misconceptions but still built a network of information upon which all future generations will depend for their civilization.

The Internet spent the first 10 years searching for an identity, in many ways. As the Internet went from being a research tool to a consumer obsession in the mid-1990s, everyone tried to get in on the act, searching for different rationales why the Internet should be big business. Media critic Douglas Rushkoff explains this evolution cogently. According to him, we've struggled with a number of misconceptions about why the Internet was important. At first, the Internet was big because it could be a channel for entertainment. They said that "content is king," as if the world was waiting for Rupert Murdoch to come put some big, popular shows on it to make it good. Next we became obsessed with "e-commerce," as if the Internet would cause all brick-and-mortar stores to shut down. When that never quite happened, there was investing online (which was a coincidence, because so many hot stocks were Internet companies). Finally, in 2001, the whole deck of cards fell apart; the tech bubble popped and people wondered if we were all excited about nothing when it came to the Internet.

Out of the ashes of our high expectations, the real fun began. According to Rushkoff, the killer app of the Internet is people—not music or investing or content, but access to other human beings. He is right. Connecting human beings to one another is the one application for which the Internet is perfect. Television and cinema were better carriers of entertainment, malls are still superior if you want to shop, but no technology is as good at connecting human beings into social networks as the Internet.

Consider the meteoric rise of MySpace.com. It offers nothing but the chance to connect to others. Its entertainment is nothing more than people being themselves. These social networks are the one Internet business that is not built on hype; whether connecting scientists collaborating about biotechnology, bass players talking about equipment, or people looking for love, the Internet has finally discovered its true purpose—to connect human beings.

Google, China, and the Next Generation of Political Values

Politics is one of the most important ways that the Internet connects people. Information technology is providing more access to—and accountability from—our leaders. Constant news, blogs, and chat rooms keep people talking about politics. The Internet we know and love is a place of freedom, but it may not stay that way unless we are vigilant.

Going back to the heady days of the early 1990s, the first mavens of the Internet were people like John Perry Barlow, who in his "Declaration of Independence of Cyberspace" said that the Internet would mean the end of the nation-state, as we knew it. According to Barlow, as life moved increasingly into the virtual realm, we could police ourselves and would not need government. Information "wants to be free," and according to these techno-optimists, we should be free, too. The Internet appears to be the ideal technology for democracy. When the Internet began, people thought they could communicate and even engage in commerce without the need for a big police force. It was benevolent anarchy!

Of course, as billions began to connect to the Internet, it couldn't remain the Wild West. Sure, you can pretty much say whatever you like online without fear of repercussion. The Internet, for the most part, guarantees freedom of speech because it does not have the capability to track people who use it.

However, when it came to commercial uses, the sheriff moved to town. Online merchants became accountable for their behavior to VeriSign, VISA, MasterCard, and the Better Business Bureau. The U.S. Federal Trade Commission began regulating online activity, pursuing those who were perpetrating fraud. The French government stepped into the world of Internet commerce by banning the sale of Nazi paraphernalia on Yahoo Auctions. Speech has remained free, but good business practices required enforcement.

As people from different cultures begin connecting to the Internet, it appears that the Internet is only as democratic as people make it. Government's next move online has been significantly less comfortable. China has recently forced Google and Yahoo to rewrite their search software so that it supports the values of state security over individual freedom by blocking certain sites. In order to continue doing business in China, the Chinese government forced Google and Yahoo to disable certain functionalities of their products so that Chinese citizens cannot connect to Web pages on topics such as human rights and democracy. You know you have entered a new phase of information technology when Secretary of

State Condoleezza Rice was forced to explain the intricacies of search-engine programming when discussing democracy.

In the future provided by small, cheap information technology, states will have even more opportunities to step in and control individual behavior. Today, for the most part, it's impossible to track the behavior of people online partly because of the relative weakness of the design of the Internet. Today's Internet is based on a network structure called Internet Protocol Version Four (IPv4), which was designed back in the 1970s and allows only a limited number of "IP addresses," the thing that shows where the computer is located on the Internet. Because of the limited number of IP addresses, many computers share the same address, which is assigned when you log onto your network. When you use the Internet, people may know that you have come from a router in your neighborhood, but they cannot track the specific machine. In addition, because you can easily "fake" an IP address, with the proper precautions it is impossible to track your individual behavior online. (Note: This freedom also allows spammers to pound your inbox with junk without being stopped. It's not all good.) Another major problem of IPv4 is that, as it stands, the United States gets over 75 percent of all the available addresses. As the Internet has grown wildly in Asia and Europe, this disparity is cramping the growth of IT in these other countries.

A new protocol is debuting around the world: IPv6. This protocol was designed to take care of the problem of too few addresses. IPv6 offers trillions of possible addresses, enough to give a website to every grain of sand on earth, and that's good news for all the other countries looking to expand their networks.

However, there are other effects. The architecture of IPv6 will provide networks with the ability to track individual packets of data and to direct them. Moreover, billions of new devices will receive their own IP addresses, right down to the individual wireless device and even the individual person. This promises a major leap ahead in security and quality of service, but there is one major difference between it and the old system—every device can be tracked. Spam will likely decrease, but the relative anonymity IPv4 provided may be gone for good.

These technologies could result in states being able to exert much greater influence through the Internet. Technology will advance to make censorship easier, even automated. Consider that China Telecom Corporation is investing US$100 million in a secure IPv6 system called ChinaNet Next Carrying Network, or CN2. Today, China's "Great Firewall" can inspect URL data and keywords such as *Falun* and intercept data entering the country. But in a nation short on IP addresses, IPv6 architecture could allow states to track such information requests right to the house, computer, and maybe the person who initiated the search. Instead of having ISPs do arcane detective work via tracing IP numbers to a neighborhood, the new technology could give governments command-and-control capabilities with greater automation than ever before.

The debate over privacy, security, democracy, and freedom has only begun.

CHECKLIST: Driving the Future of Information Technology

✔ Information technology will become more powerful and require less maintenance.

✔ Information technology is becoming so small, powerful, and cheap that it will be added to nearly any device.

✔ IT will break the class barrier—information and communications will be for poor and rich people alike.

✔ IT won't necessarily mean democracy—there will be more surveillance capability than ever before. Not every country with information technology will use it to support freedom.

IMPLICATIONS: Information Technology

1. *Cheaper, more automated IT will mean more competitors.* If you think that your big expensive IT infrastructure insulates you from smaller competitors entering your market, think again. Even more than today, small companies will get access to the tools of the big corporations, letting them compete in markets that were once off limits. Goliath, meet David.

2. *Focus on service, not technology.* Sure, RFID may help you check out of the grocery store quicker. But despite some optimistic reports on artificial intelligence, computers remain pretty dumb. The real killer app is solving people's problems—and for that, the human touch is still the best. When was the last time that an automated phone system made you feel cared for as a customer?

3. *E-commerce will be everywhere.* With the proliferation of IT in unlikely devices, just think of the number of places you can conduct electronic commerce. Out in the woods? In people's cars? The sky's the limit. Think of new places you can connect with your customers.

health care

new gadgets vs.
following doctors' orders

e are on the verge of a new era in health care. Sadly, it is not that we are about to enter a radically more efficient world where we proactively keep people healthy at a fraction of the cost. This era is expensive. Yes, we are learning more about the causes of disease and attempting all kinds of incredible procedures like face transplants. We are even exploring the use of nanotechnology to create anticancer robots that will someday float around our bloodstreams protecting us from harm. However, all this comes at a price, which is about to double. Driven by the aging of the Boomers and many

expensive new diagnostic tools, we will be spending more, all while still struggling with chronic disease.

Sticker Shock—Skyrocketing Health Care Costs Worldwide

The most important thing driving the future of health care is something you probably do not need to be told—it is phenomenally costly. The United States, just one example, spends approximately $1.9 trillion on its health care system. That figure is larger than the entire economy of nearly every country on earth. The cost of health care is rising an average of 8 percent annually, outpacing growth in wages every year for the last five. Moreover, as the Baby Boomers begin to age, that number is expected to double. America alone could be spending $4 trillion a year on health care. Given that the United States devotes 18 cents of every dollar to health care, the idea of doubling that number is daunting, especially because recent studies show we don't seem to be any healthier than those in other developed countries, like the U.K., which spends considerably less.[1]

We are facing a challenge: how to get better health outcomes without spending trillions of dollars doing it. To accomplish this, there are more than a few issues to face.

Attitudes Toward Health Care

The health care industry could soon be as reviled as tobacco companies are. How is it possible that people view an industry devoted to healing with the same suspicion they reserve for cigarette manufacturers? One is seeking cures for cancer and patching your kid up after he breaks his arm; the other is trying to addict you to a known cancer-causing product that will destroy your lungs, lead to erectile dysfunction, and increase the likelihood of a heart attack. One would think no industry's public relations could be as bad as the tobacco industry's, but think again.

Pharmaceuticals, just one part of the health care industry, are already feeling the pain. A recent Harris Consumer Poll asks consumers every year, "Do you believe the following industries have your best interest at heart?" The poll lists airlines, banks, food companies, as well as tobacco and pharmaceutical corporations. In 1997, the poll showed that the pharmaceutical industry was one of the most trusted; more than 75 percent said that pharmaceutical companies were trustworthy. Cigarette companies ranked around 30 percent.

Fast-forward to 2005. America has seen double-digit increases in health care premiums. Some people are struggling just to pay for all of their prescriptions, which often cost hundreds of dollars per month. Employers are struggling to give their employees health care benefits. Making matters worse are high-profile scandals, like the one exposed by New York Attorney General Eliot Spitzer involving GlaxoSmithKline (GSK), a drug company (for hiding data about the effects of its antidepressant Paxil). GSK was recommending that doctors prescribe the psychiatric drug to children based on one published study—all the while knowing there were four published studies that said the drug was useless. Just after the GSK scandal was resolved, Merck hit the headlines about the risk of heart attack associated with its painkiller Vioxx.

The result? In 2005, the poll showed that only 34 percent of Americans felt that pharmaceutical companies had their best interest at heart—only a few points above tobacco companies!

How will people feel if the cost of health care doubles? Ironically, we are going to need health care more than ever at a time when its cost is skyrocketing and people mistrust it.

Nanotechnology Gadgets or Pills

Given the incredible cost of health care and the burden placed on governments, employers, and individuals alike, people are starting to wonder what we, as a society, are going to do to avoid going broke. We have all seen impressive gains in the sophistication of health care. In the past 30 years alone, researchers made giant leaps toward understanding the causes and risk factors of major diseases. We have also designed revolutionary diagnostic tools, less invasive and more efficacious procedures, and incredible new pharmaceutical therapies. The expectation, naturally, is that with the new knowledge we will begin down the path toward cheaper, more effective health care. We are clever folks spending trillions of dollars; surely, we can arrive at a revolution in health.

But the answer lies somewhere between two stories, one about how health care is advancing and the other about how it is stuck in its tracks.

To advance health care, Triton Biosystems is developing a cancer smart-bomb using nanotechnology. The idea is to improve on radiation and chemotherapy, which have unpleasant side effects. So Triton is coating iron nanoparticles with antibodies that specifically target tumor cells. A doctor then applies a magnetic field to the diseased area and the iron particles heat up, killing the tumor cells and sparing the healthy tissue. Though still in development, nanotechnologies such as this could revolutionize the way we treat cancer by allowing us to find it earlier and treat it with considerably less discomfort to the patient. Although it is one of many innovations that cost millions to research and develop, it could save billions in the coming years.

This is the kind of innovation we hope will improve health care in many areas. Cancer treatment is wretched and painful. The idea of making it more effective and less painful through technology is a welcome one. If you research new technologies currently under development, you will find hundreds if not thousands that could improve care. Drugs with fewer side effects, digital information systems that reduce medical errors, new diagnostic devices that warn of diseases in their early stages—government and private industry are investing billions in researching these new technologies. One hopes it will result in a considerably better system of care.

Often, there are improvements to our health care system that do not require up-to-the-minute research into the latest technologies. People incur exorbitant costs and unnecessarily use scarce health care resources simply because they do not comply with doctors' orders. Consider the amount of money spent treating one simple foot infection.

In downtown Baltimore, a local woman came to the emergency room with a badly infected foot. Sadly, the patient was a drug addict living a hard life on the streets. She had no regular access to primary care, so she went to the emergency room when something was seriously wrong. In this case, the doctor prescribed a five-day course of oral antibiotics and discharged her.

Instead of taking the antibiotics, she sold them to buy narcotics. Antibiotics fetch a high price on the street because drug users need them to treat abscesses caused by dirty needles. The patient did not complete her course of antibiotics, and the foot did not heal properly. She later returned to the hospital, but her infection was so bad half of her foot had to be amputated. She was admitted to the hospital; the surgery was done; and, on discharge, the doctor prescribed a five-day course of antibiotics.

Once again, she sold them and her foot did not heal. She was readmitted for an overnight hospital stay. The infection came under control and she left, again with a five-day course of oral antibiotics. This repeated six times, until finally the hospital staff placed the woman under house arrest at a skilled nursing center for a week and forcibly administered IV antibiotics to clear up the infection permanently. The estimated cost of this one small foot infection, which could have been treated inexpensively, was approximately $250,000 and the partial loss of the woman's foot.

My point in relating this story is not to blame poor, addicted, miserable people for the massive cost to our health care system. It is to illustrate the fact that society faces rapidly climbing health care costs, and although we spend billions on nanotechnology, diagnostic equipment, and other important advances, doing something as seemingly simple as getting people to take their pills can save society $250,000—not to mention, in this case, saving the woman's foot and eliminating months of agony!

When thinking about the future of health care, people often want to hear that there are magic pills and magical insights into the nature of disease. There is no doubt that technology will make health care more efficient and offer treatments for conditions we were powerless to fight against in the past. Good antibiotics have only been around for a few decades; before that, millions died of infections that are easy to treat today. Many other advances can be made on various fronts, including better nutrition, better education about the importance of timely health care, compliance with doctors' instructions, better living conditions, and pollution control.

Healthy Living

Here is another forecast about health care that nobody wants to read: Doughnuts, vodka, cigarettes, and fried rice are still out. High fiber, low fat, and regular exercise are still in. You may not want to hear about it, but lifestyle modification could be the key to saving billions of dollars in health care costs.

Doctors can prescribe drugs that took billions to develop, and they can use advanced diagnostic equipment and surgical procedures, but that may not be enough to keep a person who is 150 pounds overweight and smokes two packs a day healthy. The United States is experiencing an epidemic of obesity. Despite cutesy books asserting that French and Japanese women don't get fat, statistics show that people in most industrialized nations in Europe and Asia are becoming almost as obese as those in the United States.[2] Obesity can lead to diabetes, hypertension, heart disease, stroke, vascular disease, and other negative secondary health effects.

Experts estimate the total worldwide cost of obesity in the billions. For most people, the cure for obesity is a matter of individual choice. Losing weight and stopping smoking will save lives and billions in rising health costs. The problem is that this has to be done by each individual; it is not going to be solved by a bunch of Ph.D.s in a lab somewhere. Education may help; inculcating good eating and exercise habits in children may help. As non–Space Age as it sounds, a large part of the future of health care will revolve around getting people to take the stairs and skip dessert.

As it stands, there is far more research into new drugs than there is in trying to figure out how to convince people to modify their lifestyles. Health care leaders are looking at the last few decades of "public service announcements" and trying to determine why personal health choices are increasingly leading to sedentary, unhealthy lifestyles. There is no answer yet, and much research is still required.

Increased Competition for Health Care Talent Worldwide

The health care system of the future will soon face a human resource crisis. The Provident Foundation, a nonprofit think tank that focuses on the future of health care, estimates that by 2020 America alone could be facing a shortage of 200,000 doctors and 800,000 nurses. As American health care gets more sophisticated, there will be an increasing need for specialists, yet predictions are that there will not be enough to meet the need.

For example, the new standard of care is to provide colonoscopies to all Americans at age 50, but we are running short of gastroenterologists to perform the number of procedures required. The American College of Physicians cites low rates of insurance reimbursements for colonoscopies and an increase in the number of physicians prescribing them as the main obstacles to achieving the new standard of care.[3]

Obstetrics is experiencing similar problems, although liability and high malpractice insurance premiums appear to be the key causes. The Pennsylvania Medical Society reports that more and more gynecologists are dropping obstetrics from their practice because malpractice insurance is too expensive to make it financially feasible (or desirable) to deliver babies. In some states, plaintiffs can sue obstetricians for malpractice up to 23 years after the birth of the baby.[4] The result is extremely high insurance premiums when compared to other specialties. As a result, doctors are choosing less risky specialties; cutting back on the number of procedures they do; and, in some cases, taking early retirement.

This has forced an increasing number of hospitals to turn to medical students, interns, and residents to perform deliveries. More doctors are willing to provide prenatal care and regular gynecological services, but then they tell expectant mothers to turn to whoever is on call at the hospital for the actual delivery.

As aging populations demand more health care services, not only will there be a shortage of specialists, but experts forecast four missing nurses for every missing doctor. The need for skilled nurses, nursing aides, community health workers, and others will be even greater. The human side of medicine will be in as short supply as the technical side.

Given this shortage of health care talent, you might want to invest in medical schools for African and Middle Eastern doctors. America will be competing with Europe and Asia for medical talent that will fill the thousands of jobs available. As economies improve in Asia, many trained professionals—educated in the West and elsewhere—who once came to the U.S. and Europe will remain in their home countries. Trained professionals from countries such as China, India, and Korea, which once "donated" scientific and medical talent to the West, will no longer need to flee their countries to achieve richer lives now that opportunities exist. It will no longer be as attractive to live abroad when well-paying health care jobs are available at home. There will be fierce competition for medical expertise on all levels. Encouraging young people in Africa and the Middle East, with their abundance of young people, to enter the health care professions may help meet the tremendous global demand for skilled health care workers.

Learning to Die with Dignity

With aging populations ballooning, we will need to learn to die well. Otherwise, we will pay dearly in terms of dollars and the dignity of patients. Americans have never been comfortable with death. Because our culture promotes individuality and prizes success, we motivated, ambitious Yanks almost view death as a character flaw, something that could be avoided if we really made the effort. With modern medicine, death rarely happens at home. Instead it is something that happens in a place removed from our day-to-day lives. Most of us go to a hospital only a few times in our lives, but that's where many of us die. Death remains a mysterious event we prefer not thinking about. In the next 15 to 20 years, the world is going to face the issue, especially with these trends:

- The Boomers are about to double the number of senior citizens in America, from 35 million to 70 million.

- Experts forecast that health care spending may mushroom from $2 trillion a year to $4 trillion a year.

- Most of our spending on health care comes in the last six months of life.

Dying is really expensive because of the way in which we use our health care resources. As the population ages, more people naturally will die. As much as we don't want to consider finances in times of emotional stress, to keep from breaking the bank, we will be forced to learn much more about the process. In the future we must examine the process of dying—financially, ethically, and spiritually.

The death of a family member is never easy. Today, it is intertwined with the health care system, often in the intensive care unit. Family members must decide how aggressively they want to use technology to prolong the life of the dying person. Sometimes, in the very last moments of life, the question of resuscitation arises.

Many people have watched TV shows where when somebody dies the doctors quickly apply electric paddles to the patient's chest, and *zap*, the patient wakes up. What is never mentioned is that about 90 percent of the time these patients never recover meaningfully. In addition, the process itself is undignified, resulting in cracked ribs, teeth knocked loose, and possibly months hooked up to machines.

All too often, family members under emotional duress ask hospital staff to "do everything" if the patient's heart should stop. Never mind that the patient is 84 years old with failed kidneys, congestive heart failure, out-of-control diabetes, and dementia. Because of our denial of the inevitable, we spend thousands of dollars of health care resources even when no positive outcome is possible. Instead of peacefully meeting this transition, hospitals often engage in combat during the final moments. We spare no expense and no suffering of the patient to avoid the inevitable. Often, the end is dragged out for weeks with no potential for meaningful recovery.

Clearly, this is a matter of great importance and can't be covered fully in this small space. But, until now, we have had the luxury of avoiding a frank debate on the matter. When health care costs are predicted to double in only 15 years, we will be forced to have this discussion. If the recent political outcry over the Terri Schiavo case is an indicator, we have much to talk about.

There will be an increased need for hospices. We will be able to reduce suffering and end-of-life costs by letting people know that they have options about how aggressive their treatment should be, especially in the face of overwhelming chronic and acute illness. In addition, there will be increased focus on how to meet this transition with dignity and comfort.

The Next Big Challenge: Complex Disease

Unquestionably, advances in the pharmaceutical industry have resulted in dramatically improved care. In the last 60 years, we have come to learn a great deal about the mechanisms of disease and developed treatments for illnesses from heart disease to schizophrenia. Pharmaceutical companies are suffering from bad press right now—some of it of their own making—but their contributions to our knowledge of health care are undeniable.

Their appetite for research is also undeniable. Drug development is a difficult, high-risk business. For every drug that makes it into your pharmacy, there are 10,000 compounds tested. Most fail early, but several get through and look very promising until the very end. A company can spend up to a billion dollars and still not come out with a viable product. On the other hand, when it does succeed, the result can be billions in revenue. Just think of Viagra—researchers were working on a new treatment for high blood pressure, discovered a way to dilate blood vessels, and they had a multibillion-dollar blockbuster.

Something is changing. Pharmaceutical companies have noticed that even though they are spending billions more on research than ever before, the number of new drugs submitted for approval to the Food and Drug Administration (and its worldwide equivalents) is falling. More money spent on research does not equal more and better drugs on the market. In an effort to stay competitive, drug companies are merging, combining their product lines and research dollars into behemoth companies. Still, the number of new drugs discovered is not increasing. It seems that "money in" doesn't equal "drugs out" in the way it once did. Wall Street and drug companies are confused. Is the magic gone?

Some thought leaders in health care think there is a larger issue at work: We have picked the low-hanging fruits. Experts are researching simple, single-mechanism illnesses and have designed definitive treatments. Bacterial infections that once frequently killed people are now treatable with all sorts of antibiotics. Hypothyroidism can be treated simply with a drug called Synthroid. Take Fosamax and calcium and you will stave off osteoporosis. These were not simple to discover, but the diseases they treat involve one fixable organ.

Today, some of our biggest health challenges come from complex diseases such as Alzheimer's, Parkinson's, and diabetes. Collectively these diseases cost billions. We are not sure what causes them, what all the warning signs are, or how to cure them. These are diseases for which a single pill or treatment may not be the answer. A great deal of research, at perhaps exponentially higher costs, is needed.

Take Alzheimer's disease, for instance. It is unclear what leads to this degeneration of the brain, though we know that the disease increases the cost of caring for the affected person many times over. Scientists have discovered that grey amyloid plaque builds up in the brains of people with Alzheimer's, but they are not certain if the plaque causes Alzheimer's or if Alzheimer's causes the plaque. There appear to be many risk factors for the disease, from stress to exposure to aluminum.

Science has spent billions on studying Alzheimer's, but due to its complex nature, a cure or even an effective treatment is not available. This may be a harbinger of the problems and costs associated with future drug development. Years go by, and although we have become accustomed to regular improvements in the technologies of care, we may be entering a period where the next great leap ahead in health care may take a while. This is another reason to focus on healthy lifestyles and doing the most with the resources we've already committed.

o   o   o

Health care is one of the greatest challenges facing the planet, and when people are spending trillions of dollars on it, there are certainly enormous issues that will affect its future. In this chapter, we have looked at just a few of the drivers affecting health care; countless other issues will affect the world. Among them are how to provide access to drugs to all those who need them and how to provide health care to the increasing number of people who are uninsured.

CHECKLIST: Driving the Future of Health Care

✔ Health care costs are increasing at a terrific rate.

✔ Most people dislike and distrust the U.S. health system.

✔ Technology could dramatically improve the cost and access problems of health care, but so could simply complying with doctors' orders.

✔ Healthy lifestyles will still be a key factor in cutting cost and increasing well-being.

✔ A shortage of doctors and nurses creates competition worldwide.

✔ Already high malpractice could further reduce the number of specialists needed.

✔ Learning to die well will be an important topic as the Boomers force the issue on us.

✔ The health care industry has treated or cured many "simple" diseases, and now it must tackle complex diseases that are harder to treat.

IMPLICATIONS: Health Care

1. *Every dollar spent on health care is an opportunity.* Sure, the upcoming challenges in health care seem daunting. Don't forget that this is a great market opportunity as well. Both large *and* small businesses can develop goods and services for the trillions of dollars in market needs. Whether you help people organize their medications, invent a better bandage, or create a service to find nurses, there are endless opportunities to keep people healthy while reducing waste.

2. *We'll need to redesign everything to promote health, or go broke.* One thing is clear: Prevention is far cheaper than the current system of medical care. To save on scarce health care resources, all of our social systems, from city planning to workplace rules, will need to

encourage health rather than just increase our already high spending. Cities will need to be redesigned to encourage physical activity and minimize stressful time in the car. Workplaces will be required to find ways to allow employees to stay active during the day. This is going to require lots of work—think about what opportunities will be made available.

3. *If you figure out a way to help people make healthy choices, you're a bazillionnaire.* For decades there have been public health campaigns that tell you to stop being unhealthy. Don't overeat. Don't drink too much. Stop smoking. Lay off the McDonald's. Everybody knows that stuff, yet the trends indicate that our bodies are paying the price for unhealthy choices. Whatever you are selling, if you can determine how to market health without wagging your finger the same old way, success awaits.

4. *Get ready to deal with more chronically sick workers.* While we make this transition from "sick care" to "health promotion," we've still got to deal with the issue of caring for those with complex, chronic diseases. Workplaces should consider how to deal with a workforce trying to live with chronic diseases. With increases in diabetes, morbid obesity, asthma, chronic obstructive pulmonary disease, and Parkinson's, the workforce will have more people who need assistance in their daily lives.

CHAPTER ELEVEN

biotechnology

scratching the surface
of the secrets of life

I f you are looking at the future, you have to consider the rapid advances in biotechnology and wonder: Will we soon be able to custom order superbabies? Will we be able to clone ourselves and send for duplicate parts as ours wear out?

Without even talking about the ethical issues behind these questions, scientifically, the answer is maybe. First will come the technologies to eliminate or repair congenital heart defects, drugs based on an individual's genetic makeup, corn that grows well in salty water, plants that can manufacture specialty plastics, and goats that can mass produce spider silk in their milk.

The possibilities seem limitless.

Discoveries in different branches of the basic sciences have driven the scientific advances of the past two centuries. Nineteenth-century advances came largely in chemistry. We discovered how chemicals interact. We invented the steam engine. We advanced our knowledge of metalworking and explosives. Our knowledge of chemistry led us to know the basic origins of disease. The result was the industrial revolution and advances in public health.

Physics was the technology driving the twentieth century. We explored the physical realm at every level, from particle physics to astrophysics. Throughout the century we discovered how to manipulate radiation, waves, and electrons. This led us to astounding innovations in communications, energy, and weapons technology—everything from radio and television, X-ray and CAT scan diagnostics, to nuclear power and nuclear bombs. We even learned more about our place in the universe through astrophysics.

The twenty-first century may be the century of biotechnology. We are trying to understand how nature does things. The possibilities are bright, although we are just scratching the surface. We are genetically engineering organisms to produce precisely the characteristics we desire. Researchers are learning how to read human genomes to design drugs tailored to an individual's specific needs. We're even helping nature develop more precise efficient ways of manufacturing things ("biomanufacturing"). The most important thing about biotechnology is that we have barely begun to understand or make use of the power it holds, and we will need a vigorous debate on the ethical implications of some of these possibilities.

Biotech: The Tip of the Iceberg

Genetics is another area in which, despite the headlines, we have barely begun to unlock the possibilities. It turns out that life is complex and Mother Nature guards her secrets carefully. There was, briefly, a belief shared by scientists, businesspeople, and investors that genetic research had brought us to the cusp of the ability to control life. We've learned a great deal, but the problem is more complex than they thought, and we've got a ways to go.

Let's step back in time to the late 1990s. The Internet technology boom was in full swing. Dot-com companies were flush with cash. Techno-optimism was the order of the day. Pharmaceutical companies were making enormous amounts of money, and the health care industry was becoming increasingly excited over the possibilities of biotech.

There was much to be excited about. The Human Genome Project was nearing completion. People expected that once it was finished, pharmaceutical developers would understand which genes created which proteins and would then invent thousands of new drugs targeted right at the root of each disease. The sky was the limit for biotech.

In the year 2000, Craig Venter, president of Celera Genomics, and Francis Collins, from the National Human Genome Research Institute, announced that they had completed their human genes database and sequenced the entire human DNA code. This was an immense scientific achievement that holds enormous implications for humanity. Teams of scientists all over the world identified all three billion chemically based pairs of the genome, which holds approximately 35,000 genes. Like a kid on Christmas Day, the world awaited the recipe for human life.

What we heard was probably more fascinating, but disappointing because there is much more work to be done before we know quite how the genome functions. We have yet to understand how this discovery can be put to practical use. The genes in the human genome do not create human tissue in a linear fashion. One gene does not necessarily code one protein; instead the products of those genes, amino acids, interact in a complex manner and combine at different times to create proteins and tissues.

The life sciences offer vast new frontiers. We have learned an amazing amount in just the last decade. However, to reap the true promise of these sciences—defeating disease, slowing aging, reducing suffering around the world—we have a long way to go.

That isn't to say that we're not advancing.

The Impact of Biotechnology on Agriculture: Greater Yield

The Monsanto Company began commercializing its genetically modified crops with special traits in the 1990s, giving farmers new capabilities and changing the business model of farming. This has created a huge debate over the issue of who owns life.

Genetic engineering can alter plants to produce bigger fruit, do better in dry climates, or resist certain pests. This is a successful technology. In the past decade, acreage devoted to genetically modified plants grew at double-digit rates, to 222 million acres.[1]

There are many benefits to engineered crops, especially in developing economies such as those of China, India, and Brazil. Small cotton farmers, for example, are cultivating engineered crops that grow more cotton with less chemical pesticide. The increased efficiency of agricultural production in turn often alleviates malnutrition and environmental damage. Life sciences are also improving the nutritional content of food, reducing the need for pesticides and allowing food to grow in poorer soil with a higher content of saline or brackish water.

Still, the ethical issues of genetically modified crops have yet to be resolved. For the first time in human history, farming is subject to intellectual property law. Biotech companies own the patents to their modified genomes, and the business model often charges royalties for the use of the seeds. This is a significant departure from traditional agriculture, where producers modify seeds for greater hardiness and store them for the next season. In addition, once farmers transition to genetically modified crops, they may lose their stores of seed in a few seasons, which could mean that once you start buying engineered seeds you may not be able to stop. For farmers eking out a subsistence living, this is a real conundrum.

Critics of genetically modified foods fear that increasing the use of these branded, corporately engineered seeds will make subsistence farmers dependent on foreign companies, when previously they were able to plant, crossbreed, harvest, and save seeds, using techniques that have been around for millennia.

TRADING BETTER YIELD FOR A DISRUPTIVE NEW BUSINESS MODEL

There are also legal ramifications. Monsanto has sued farmers for "illegally using" its seeds. For example, the company's Roundup Ready seeds feature a genetic modification that makes plants herbicide resistant. One farmer in Canada used the seed to raise a genetically modified crop. The pollen blew into his neighbor's field, and when Monsanto tested neighboring crops to see if farmers were "stealing" their intellectual property, the pollen contamination made it appear that the farmer had stolen patented seeds. The Canadian court agreed with Monsanto's claim, which led to wide debate about the ethics of biotech agriculture.

As our abilities in biotechnology grow, we will need to assess not only whether we can do something, but also whether we should. The business of agriculture is tied into the history of civilization itself. Suddenly shifting toward the model of paying for designer seeds could have environmental and social effects. With every biotechnology, we will need to decide whether the added yield is worth the effect on the farmers themselves.

The Impact of Biotechnology on Pharmaceuticals: Personalized Medications

Pharmaceutical companies are using biotechnology in a number of ways that will improve health care. One of the most exciting developments is called *pharmacogenomics* or, in lay terms, a "personalized drug program." Our expanding understanding of genetics is giving drug companies clues to which pill is right for an individual based on that person's genetic makeup.

For this reason, there are often several drugs in the same class of therapy; for example, there are several proton pump inhibitors used for heartburn, including Nexium, Prevacid, and Aciphex. Statins, which control cholesterol, include Lipitor, Crestor, and Zocor. Although each drug employs roughly the same mechanism of action, they vary slightly. Sometimes it takes trial and error to determine which will be right for you. Pharmaceutical researchers describe people as *responders*, *nonresponders*, or *superresponders*, depending upon their reactions to a given medication. The dilemma today is that doctors can't tell what an individual's response will be until he or she tries the drug.

That may soon change. Pharmaceutical researchers are using biotechnology to distinguish between you and me to determine which drug each of us should take. They have discovered that genetic variations among people affect their responses to a drug. As a result, genetically targeted medicines may soon be available.

One of the first such drugs is BiDil, a treatment for heart failure. BiDil is specified for use in African-American patients. Initial studies showed that Caucasians had little or no response to the drug, but African-American populations responded positively. Further study proved that the drug was especially effective in treating African-Americans—it reduced mortality by 43 percent and reduced the time to first hospitalization due to heart failure by 39 percent.

Today, many researchers are collecting the genomes of participants in drug trials, with the goal of one day correlating the information about who takes a medicine and who responds best to it. Further studies seem likely to find other drugs that can target specific populations.

Advances in Biomanufacturing: Nature as Factory

Today's manufacturing is impressive. Taking plastic, glass, and metal to make a laptop computer takes sophistication, but you have to admit, nature is more clever. Our bodies can take *chicken and potatoes;* rearrange the molecules; and produce muscle, bone, and nerve tissue. Now *that's* advanced manufacturing. Thus, one of the most radical applications of biotechnology is in developing the ability to engineer organisms that will manufacture things for us in the same way living organisms do.

Take, for example, the goat. Working in a factory, goats are pretty useless. They show up late, wander around all day, and maybe eat the garbage, but working *as the factory itself,* scientists are finding the goat very handy. Nexia Biotechnologies has produced a material called BioSteel for medical, military, and industrial applications. BioSteel is a biologically produced version of spider silk, which has surprising applications in items such as surgical bandages and bulletproof vests. It is made by transplanting the silk genes from orb-weaving spiders into goats, which are then bred to produce spider silk in their milk, from which the protein is extracted.

There are other materials we are hoping to make using biomanufacturing. Several companies are looking at ways to produce plastics without using petroleum. Archer Daniels Midland is launching a farm that will grow PHA, a flexible type of polymer, in corn. The plant in Clinton, Iowa, will produce 50,000 tons of biodegradable plastics for use in coatings and film, blown fibers, adhesives, and many other products. An added benefit is that this type of plastic will be biodegradable, unlike petroleum-based polymers.

Today's technology is sophisticated; tomorrow's technology could be positively elegant. Instead of sheep simply producing wool, livestock may produce pharmaceuticals or cell-based computer parts. How's that for a revolution in agriculture?

Lower Cost: Greater Advances

The falling price of the equipment needed to sequence and manipulate genes will lead to even greater advances, which, in turn, will lead to greater benefits to society, particularly health care. We will be able to sequence genes in more places for more purposes.

The increasing power and falling prices of biotech equipment is largely the result of advances in information technology. Moore's Law (see Chapter 9) functions in biotechnology, too, and the better the computers, the faster we can sequence and analyze genes. Coupled with advances in nanotechnology (see Chapter 13), such as the anticipated ultrasmall DNA-profile device, a "lab on a chip," as it is called, these innovations are expected to cut the cost of usable biotechnology significantly.

Currently, sequencing a genome is expensive. In 2004, the National Human Genome Research Institute set a goal of sequencing a human genome for the low, low price of $100,000. (Compare this to the original price tag of $3 billion to sequence the first genome.) Its longer-term goal is to get the cost of sequencing a genome down to $1,000. Once it goes below that level, doctors will be able to run genomic screens on their patients routinely. Once we understand the genome of every patient, we will be able to personalize treatment plans.

Prior to cracking open the human genome, the hope was that we would instantly understand a person's genome; figure out which genes were likely to cause disease; and, it was hoped, fix them through gene therapy. Now that we understand how complex genetics and diseases really are, we have different goals. At least initially, we may not be able to tell instantly if a given person will get a specific disease. Genomics instead promises the ability to identify genetic risk factors for such diseases as diabetes, Alzheimer's, and heart disease. Of course, these are simply risk factors; if your lifestyle and the environment are favorable, you may never have the disease. Like many things, illness is a mix of your genes and your environment.

The ability to sequence a genome inexpensively could change how medicine is approached over your entire lifetime. Today, health care is really "sick care"; we wait for people to get sick and then try to help them. It is probable that in about 15 years doctors will be able to sequence your genome when you are young and tell you your biggest risk for disease. That way, doctors will be able to make a plan for you early, before you get sick.

Let's say you have a family history of heart disease. When you are 28, your doctor might say, "Based on your genome, we're not going to wait until you have high cholesterol before we worry about heart trouble. You need to keep your cholesterol at 70 and exercise regularly starting today, or you have a 72 percent chance of having a massive coronary at age 40."

I might get the same talk about preventing disease, but my plan would be about my family's risk of diabetes. Instead of waiting for illness or trying to be saints—eating nothing but fish, soy protein, and oat bran—we can have a *health* care plan that prevents disease throughout our lives. It's better than waiting for a crippling stroke or massive heart attack before we change our habits.

Is Biotechnology Playing God? The Possibilities and the Upcoming Ethical Debate

You may have seen some amazing photos of biotech experiments. One of the most stunning is the image of a mouse with a human ear growing on its back. Less disturbing is Dolly, the cloned Scottish sheep.

It's one thing, some say, to design rice that is more nutritious, but cloning mammals, growing ears of one species onto another species—these are the stories that make splashy headlines and stimulate a much-needed ethical debate. Obviously, we have achieved a certain amount of technological power to alter the life around us. For a variety of reasons, including religious and ethical concerns, not everyone agrees this is a good thing. Others ask if we are ready to handle that power and question the consequences of our new abilities. To make intelligent decisions, we need to determine which capabilities make us the most nervous and discuss what is really coming in the field of biotechnology.

STEM CELLS

Embryonic stem cell research is causing a major political stir, particularly in the United States. As touchy as the subject is, especially to abortion opponents, stem cells offer tremendous possibilities for curing or helping us prevent certain diseases. There are all kinds of stem cells, but embryonic stem cells seem to retain the ability to contribute to 200 or so different tissues, and scientists can therefore use them to repair or replace those tissues (it is unclear whether adult or umbilical cord stem cells have this capacity). Eventually, we may be able to create new tissues from our own stem cells, ensuring the ability to replace worn-out, diseased, or otherwise damaged tissue with new tissue that matches perfectly (because it is your own, thereby eliminating the risk of rejection). Some therapies already use this method.

For example, studies show that transplanting stem cells into the brain reduces the effects of Parkinson's disease by helping the brain regrow cells to replace those that have stopped producing dopamine.[2] Alzheimer's disease may be amenable to this technique as well. If we can advance the philosophical discussion about stem cells, tremendous progress can be made.

CLONING

As is the case with the stem cell debate, most people worldwide reject the idea of human "reproductive" cloning. It looks like most people are uninterested in a world where we could make perfect copies of ourselves, especially because animals cloned this way have high incidences of cancer, arthritis, and other diseases. However, the techniques learned over the last 50 years of experimenting with cloning could lead to cures for disease.

Scientists hope that one day "therapeutic cloning" will generate tissues and organs for such things as liver transplants. If they can clone a new liver from a person's own DNA, the body would be less likely to reject it. Researchers have been developing a way to grow these new organs in pigs, which could be harvested for use by humans. Scientists chose pigs because pig tissues and organs are the most like human tissues and organs. In addition, scientists have figured out how to deactivate the genes that cause pigs' bodies to reject transplanted organs. This process of growing an organ in one species for use in humans is called *xenotransplantation.*

The idea of regularly growing tissue in one species for use in humans is an example of the ethical issues we have only begun to discuss, although the practice of mixing the tissues of multiple species has been done. For example, scientists have transplanted baboon hearts, but that was in the case of extreme illness and the procedure is very rare. The techniques are not yet perfected, so we should start this debate early. There is a lot to talk about.

The root question is how we define human life. Is a collection of cells, a blastocyte, a human being even if the cells were never placed in a human body? Is a tissue human if it comes from our genes but wasn't germinated in a human body? As our abilities advance, so too does the need for in-depth discussion of medical ethics.

CHECKLIST: Driving the Future of Biotechnology

✔ We're at the tip of the iceberg when it comes to the power of biotech.

✔ Biotech lets us customize crops to improve yield, reduce pollution, and improve nutrition, but the disruption to the traditional business model of farming may have a negative effect in poor countries.

✔ A better understanding of the human genome will lead to medicine, drugs, and health regimens that are designed specifically for an individual's genetic makeup.

✔ We are learning to use organisms to manufacture materials such as pharmaceuticals and plastics.

✔ Some of the most promising technologies may come from stem cells and cloning, and it is likely that we will have new insights into diseases and powerful new therapies, but the ethical debate needs to happen early.

IMPLICATIONS: Biotech

1. *Consider products that can be customized to a person's genetics.* As we learn more about the role of genetics and genomics, each person will know more precisely which diseases they risk. It won't be an absolute predictor of

the future, as environment plays a role, but your genes will show your relative risk of cancer, diabetes, Alzheimer's, and other diseases. People will then want foods, drugs, and health programs designed for their genetic needs. For these reasons, keep an eye on the potential applications of biotechnology—it may change your plans for product development.

2. *Prepare for the ethical choices that will come from knowing more about genetics.* Advances in biotech will give some businesses tough dilemmas. Imagine you are an insurance company, and there is suddenly a much more accurate way of reading someone's genome to see what kind of diseases that person could likely contract due to genetics. Do you insure him? Charge him extra? What about hiring decisions? If you have two equally qualified applicants, but one knows from a genome sequence that he's twice as likely to get cancer in his forties, who gets hired? Does he keep it a secret? What if the employer discovers these things? Decide your organization's ethical framework early to prepare for these kinds of unprecedented questions.

CHAPTER TWELVE

energy

getting more
out of less

T he world will demand significantly more energy in the decades to come. No magic technology on the horizon promises limitless clean energy, but new designs can emphasize efficiency to get more out of the system already in place. Moreover, energy will become greener over time with the addition of renewable sources such as solar power, wind, and biomass. That said, energy isn't becoming green and renewable fast enough. The way we make and use energy is cutting us off from the future, resulting in pollution and climate change that could throw our ecosystem out of balance.

In the coming decades, we will be searching for ways to fill the world's hunger for reliable power, while trying to reduce environmental impact along the way. This is not significantly different from past challenges, but we're about to be doing it for six billion people and counting.

Accelerating Demand

The global demand for energy is increasing. Energy is the alpha and the omega of the future; nothing else happens without it. Do you want to see the future of IT and health care? Unplug everything. Now, how does it look? Pretty Stone Age, I'd venture. Not much nanotechnology without power, either.

The world is becoming more urbanized and more industrialized, and that requires energy. As economies industrialize, people demand cars, factories, air-conditioning, electricity for the home, and other comforts. For example, the large, populous nations of Asia, such as China and India, are demanding electricity for their cities and fuel for their automobiles. It is inevitable that industrializing nations will demand more energy to improve their lives, and under the circumstances, they may not care about where they get it. This will be a sore spot as the three billion people who have routinely dirty water and no electricity look for the comfort and safety that modernity brings.

According to Rory Stear, CEO of the Freeplay Energy Group, a socially and environmentally conscious energy-technology company, electricity means more to people than just refrigeration and lighting. When reliable electric power reaches a rural, poor area, education, jobs, and social justice follow soon after. The major question, especially in terms of the environment, is, How will these new nations power their industrial revolution? The answer is not always the most environmentally sensitive one.

With over a billion people and a rapidly developing industrial sector, China is looking toward a broad mix of ways to power its growth. Most important is coal. China has plans for 544 new coal plants to power its future.[1] Nearly 80 percent of its energy comes from coal, twice what the average country uses. India is currently the world's sixth-largest energy consumer (not a surprise, with over one billion inhabitants). Still suffering power outages due to a lack of supply, the country is looking in the short term to secure its oil supply. As it stands, India has 17 percent of the world's population, but only 0.8 percent of the known energy reserves.[2] Other industrializing nations, such as those in sub-Saharan Africa, are also seeking more sophisticated energy systems to power development. There will be a rapidly increasing demand for energy around the world, as well as heavy competition for reserves of fuel.

Efficiency: The Future of Energy

Like in health care, people looking at the future would love to hear that some clever technological innovation would solve this juggernaut of a problem—for example, that cold fusion will be here by 2020 or that a new supermaterial could be laid over the world's highways so cars could run inexpensively. Then our petroleum woes would be over.

However, no magic bullet will solve our energy problems. As billions of people seek energy from limited resources, in the future, we need to get more work out of less energy while we reduce pollution and greenhouse gas emissions. This is similar to hearing that the only way to lose weight is to eat right and exercise more, a prescription based on old wisdom, but one that requires effort and doesn't leverage any new powerful technology that will relieve us of the consequences of our actions. However, it seems that, barring any amazing new technology, we are going to have to rely on both increased efficiency and finding new supplies of energy. I hope that the world's engineers will keep looking for magic fixes, but in the meantime we need to examine forecasts for efficiency and examine the supplies we do have available.

In the industrialized world, efficiency is marginal at best. The good news is that since the energy crisis of the 1970s we have steadily become more energy efficient. Total primary energy use per capita in the United States is almost identical to what it was in 1973. Over the same period, GDP per capita increased 74 percent. National energy intensity, the energy use per unit of GDP, fell 42 percent between 1973 and 2000.[3] In other words, we are getting a bigger bang for the energy buck.

The bad news is that this relative increase in GDP compared with energy consumption has not slaked our thirst for fossil fuels nor reduced our dependence on foreign sources of oil. Despite many gains in technology in recent decades, energy efficiency is not one of the great stories of innovation. There is a considerable amount of room for improvement when it comes to making the U.S. more energy efficient, even using the same technologies. For example, Japan has twice the per-person energy efficiency of the U.S.—Japan consumes only 4.03 equivalent tons of oil per capita per year of primary energy, half of the U.S. consumption rate of 7.88 equivalent tons per capita per year.[4] Since the first oil crisis, Japan's policies have made it as energy efficient as possible. The Land of the Rising Sun is a powerhouse in science and manufacturing but has little in terms of natural resources it can trade and, therefore, is hypervigilant about controlling the amount of energy it uses. (It is perhaps no surprise that America, a larger nation with much more to trade, is less concerned about efficiency.) By comparing Japan and the United States, we can see that it is possible to guide how much energy we use through policies and design.

Why Cars Are So Fuel Inefficient

Some key energy-efficiency indicators are sadly stagnant when it comes to automobiles. For instance, the average fuel economy of a car leaves much to be desired. Despite 40 years of engineering, Detroit, Seoul, Frankfurt, and Tokyo continue to sell cars that get 20 miles per gallon. Let us not even discuss the sport utility vehicle. Unlike many environmental types who feel SUVs are satanic, I do not ascribe to any moral judgment about driving a 4x4. To me, it is just another car that goes on asphalt-paved roads. (And, let us remember, no matter what kind of car you drive, the environmental impact of building roads is the same.) SUVs can be handy in the winter. However, I am shocked that anyone would want a twenty-first-century car that gets 1970s gas mileage. One of my favorite tirades on this subject came from Mark Morford, a columnist for the *San Francisco Gate*, who noted that even the VW Dasher, an artifact of 1970s auto design and a horrible little car by most accounts, got more than 30 miles per gallon, better than many designs today.[5] There is still tremendous room for improvement.

Car companies are coming around, however slowly. The past few years have been instructive, showing automakers that consumers actually do like fuel-efficient cars. Sales of the Toyota Prius are brisk; the cars are in short supply even after two years on the market. Honda now offers several models—notably the Accord, the Civic, and the Insight. Automakers are jumping on this trend. *BusinessWeek* reported on several hybrids in development, from strange-looking pod cars right up to Lexus sedans.[6] One, the Daihatsu UFE III (it stands for Ultra-Fuel Economy, for good reason) gets 168 miles to the gallon, and a recent start-up called Accelerated Composites is planning a low-cost hybrid, manufactured in California, that will get 330 miles to the gallon and sell for around $20,000.

Of course, the latest, most-advanced designs show just how far we can push fuel efficiency. The winner of the Shell Eco-Marathon competition was the team from Lycée La Joliverie, a French high school. Its hydrogen-powered vehicle traveled at an astounding 2,730 km/liter, or over 6,400 miles per gallon. One gallon of fuel would get you from Vancouver to Boston and back. Clearly, there is a future that focuses on getting more travel out of less fuel.

Diversifying the Mix of Energy Sources

Instead of being driven only by fossil fuels, biomass, wind, solar power, water, and geothermal energy are increasingly a part of the global energy supply. The question is how fast we can increase these options while meeting the needs of growing economies.

FOSSIL FUELS ARE HERE TO STAY

Fossil fuels—petroleum, natural gas, and coal—will continue to be the backbone of world energy supplies. Hydrocarbons are chock full of energy, they travel easily in liquid or solid form, and a distribution system is already in place. When you imagine a world of fuel cells or solar-powered automobiles, ask yourself, "What are we going to do with the trillions of dollars in petroleum tankers, refineries, trucks, and gas stations?" You can't just take trillions of dollars of stuff to the dump when you are through with it.

The two major drawbacks of fossil fuels are their effects on global warming and the possibility that *cheap* oil will no longer exist. There is plenty of oil left to extract, but it will become increasingly difficult to discover new sources. Currently, for every barrel of oil we discover, we consume two. We are getting better at discovering oil, but it is getting harder to find. As one oil company executive said, "Imagine you are locked in a room full to the brim with peanuts. It's all you have to eat, but you are literally up to your neck in peanuts. When does it get tough to find peanuts? When do you start starving?"

As I tried to imagine the gastrointestinal distress, he answered the riddle. "You don't stop finding peanuts when you are out of peanuts; it's when you have eaten *half the peanuts in the room.* Because all the peanut shells surround you, it gets harder and harder to find those you *haven't* eaten. Even when you go to a place where you always find oil, you constantly come up with those old shells. Although there might be peanuts everywhere, the days of easy peanut eating are over." As much as the world loves Texas Tea (light sweet crude oil), prices may increase over time just because it is harder and harder to find new sources of it.

Let's not neglect coal as a fossil fuel. It's the industrialized world's dirty secret, handy, plentiful, easy to transport, and very useful for running electrical plants. When people think coal, they see visions of Newcastle or West Virginia miners back at the turn of the century. Most people do not realize the importance that coal still has for the world energy system. (When was the last time somebody said, "That war is just blood for coal!")

Oddly enough, coal could be the fossil fuel of the future. Supply is plentiful and reliable. According to the U.S. Department of Energy, there are about one trillion tons of coal left around the world, enough to last 180 years.[7] Given the supply, demand for coal is expected to double worldwide by 2030, from 5.4 billion short tons up to 10.6 short tons. Much of this growth is expected to come from developing economies. China, desperately searching for a way to power its rapidly industrializing economy, is rich in coal. Along with India, the two countries are forecast to be responsible for more than 85 percent of the increase in coal consumption.

What about the effects of all the black soot? A fair question if China and India are going to run their two-billion-person industrial revolution on coal. Actually, there is significant investment in technologies that could allow coal to burn far cleaner than ever before, while still producing energy at a competitive price. The FutureGen plant is a billion-dollar research project sponsored by the U.S. Department of Energy. The Department of Energy expects the plant to be online by 2012 and to feature zero-pollution emissions and a secondary output of hydrogen. Not only will the plant produce electricity without noxious by-products, but it will also supply hydrogen for fuel cells. The fuel cells will run in next-generation automobiles that will emit only steam and clean water as exhaust.

THE FUTURE OF NUCLEAR POWER

Despite the waste and the weaponry, nuclear power has a strong future. Nuclear power will increase as a source of energy, especially in Asia. The West has certainly slowed in its support of nuclear energy since the days of Ready Kilowatt, who in TV commercials of the 1950s touted the benefits of nuclear power as "electricity too cheap to meter!" I think we can all agree that that is one forecast that was off the mark.

There are currently 430 operating nuclear power plants around the world.[8] They supply 35 percent of Europe's total energy mix and 16 percent of all energy worldwide. Although America hasn't ordered a new plant since the 1970s, Korea and China have been ordering lots of them. Around 2004, China announced the construction of at least 30 nuclear power plants, and these will feature state-of-the art safety technology, perhaps even spurring the U.S. and Europe to increase their reliance on that supply of energy. In addition, new plants are safer and produce less waste. It is possible that nuclear power will become more popular as oil gets more difficult to find.

SOLAR POWER

Ah, the dream of the 1970s is almost realized! Solar cells on every house, getting off "the grid." Of course, everybody notices that solar energy is cheap and plentiful, and the mantra of many energy forecasts is, "By 20XX, solar energy will compete with fossil fuels." The reality is that few expect solar power to compete strongly with hydrocarbons in the near future. The "Risø Energy Report" from Denmark's Risø Energy Laboratory estimates that by 2050 solar power will become an "increasing part" of the energy portfolio.[9] Al Hegburg and Frank Verrastro, energy experts at Washington, D.C.'s Center for Strategic International Studies, project that by 2025 solar-energy use will increase, but at the same rate as fossil fuels.[10] Overall, it is widely agreed that the sun is a source of energy we would love to harness, but there are few forecasts that show that solar power could overtake hydrocarbons.

The recent increase in fuel prices is spurring many to reconsider solar energy to defray the cost of other sources. Germany is paying a premium for solar energy in an effort to wean itself from fossil fuels. Homeowners are putting panels on their homes; it has gotten to the point that solar companies are having trouble keeping enough panels in stock. As Phil Lawes, president of Insoltech Solar, recently informed me, "When fossil fuels were cheap, the problem was finding customers for solar panels. Now the problem is getting a supplier who has panels! People are finally waking up to the idea that we are addicted to oil. They want other options."

There will be advances in photovoltaic (PV) cells, which is currently the main technology used to capture solar energy, that could increase their use. Researchers at Penn State are using highly ordered titanium nanotube arrays to increase the amount of energy from PV cells. According to Craig Grimes, professor of electrical engineering at Penn State, "If we could successfully shift its band gap into the visible spectrum we would have a commercially practical means of generating hydrogen by solar energy. It beats fighting wars over Middle-Eastern oil."[11] Most energy futurists expect solar power to be a thin yet increasing slice of the global energy supply in the years to come.

WIND POWER

Wind power will produce an increasing proportion of world energy supplies. Wind power is growing an average of 30 percent a year, though from a very small base compared to fossil fuels, according to John Lawton, former chief executive of the Natural Environment Research Council.[12] Ironically, even an ecologically benign technology such as wind can generate concerns about noise and damage to bird populations. Wind power still tends to be unreliable unless you live in a place where there is constant wind. In addition, some think wind farms are unsightly, limiting wind's contribution to the global energy supply.

OCEAN POWER

A new option in renewable energy is wave power. It relies on offshore buoys that convert waves into mechanical energy, generate DC current, and then transmit it back to shore through underwater cables. Hawaii and New Jersey recently deployed ocean power systems, drawn by a desire for more renewable energy, and unwilling or unable to develop wind farms, solar farms, or biomass to meet this need. Additional development will be necessary, but some energy experts believe that ocean power may have more potential as a source of renewable energy than either solar or wind power.

Role of New Technologies

Even though new technologies are not promising us a panacea that will save us from the consequences of our actions, materials science, information technology, and advances in engineering may use innovative designs instead of cold fusion.

Buildings are the next major consumers of energy after transportation, and new designs promise new levels of energy efficiency. There is a new standard, LEED (Leadership in Energy and Environmental Design),[13] that is a mix of energy efficiency, green materials, low indoor pollution, and design that minimizes impact on the environment around the building. The City of Chicago recently announced that it would construct all its future buildings around LEED standards, so future development would not add to environmental problems.

A major component of efficiency is in heating and cooling buildings. Older buildings are not efficiently insulated and simply leak energy. One of the key issues is how to leapfrog technologies and design to update older devices and structures. New buildings may have efficiency designed into them, but how can older structures be updated, especially in places like Europe and Asia, where a disposable culture is incompatible with historical treasures? This is the territory of experts like Chris Benedict, RA, a New York architect well known for her energy-efficient designs and expertise in retrofitting buildings for energy efficiency. She makes homes in New York City up to 80 percent more energy efficient by using environmental materials and designs such as passive solar heating, high-performance windows, and low-flow plumbing.

Energy—we can't stop people from wanting it, but we can progress so that we can get more from less, as well as from less destructive sources.

CHECKLIST: Driving the Future of Energy

✔ Rapid growth in developing economies leads to increased demand for energy of all kinds, especially fossil fuels.

✔ Increased scarcity, resulting from more demand than discovery, could lead to a world of petroleum haves and have-nots. Industrialized nations could pay the price for oil, while the growth of developing countries stalls because they are competing with bigger countries.

✔ Design for greater efficiency may be more important to energy sustainability than new technologies.

✔ New materials and increased innovation spur wind, biomass, and solar power, gradually making renewable energy a viable option.

IMPLICATIONS: Energy

1. *A global supply chain may not last forever.* Many businesses are pretty used to producing things in China, assembling them in Mexico, and selling them in the United States. That assumes that petroleum is pretty cheap. That assumption may not hold out much longer. If energy for transportation gets much more expensive, would you have to completely revise your supply chain? Think local. Globalization may be too expensive, soon.

2. *Look at life-cycle costs when it comes to renewable energy.* Yes, it's a 1970s idea, but back in the first environmentalist movement, people selling "green" architecture said, "Sure, it's a little more expensive up front, but in the long run, it's cheaper." The global supply of energy will be under increasing demand from China and India,

and global warming isn't going anywhere. Look again at redesigning your buildings for energy efficiency. Choosing new office space? Consider a green building. If energy prices go up, it could mean a profitable, competitive edge.

nanotechnologies

smaller is better

For thousands of years, man's achievements were measured by their grandeur: the Pyramids, Machu Picchu, and Hoover Dam. Large, imposing edifices said to the world that you were able to achieve things beyond the dreams of mortals. In the next 10 years, what will matter is how small you make something. The era of nanotechnology is upon us. Humankind is gaining the capacity to manipulate matter at the level of one billionth of a meter, and we may be able to change our built environment in the most fundamental way since the development of tools. It may be a long time before we reap the benefits and dangers of these technologies, but if even a fraction of the hype is true, there will be serious change.

Building from the Bottom Up

Nanotechnology is letting us design materials from the molecular level on up to be exactly as we want them to be. Many scientists believe we are on the brink of a new age of industry. As sophisticated as manufacturing has become, we are still creating goods in what some describe as "a barbaric way." According to nanotech visionary K. Eric Drexler, author of *Engines of Creation* and *Nanosystems*, prenanotechnology industry is little more than smashing molecules together and hoping for the best.

That essentially is the nature of modern chemistry, metallurgy, and materials science. We take the principles of nature we assume to be true, put the molecules in one place, and bang them together. We mix up raw materials and assume a chemical reaction will result in forming new molecules (chemistry). We scrape molecules of one substance against molecules of another and end up with only the parts we want (metalworking, carving, or construction). These processes are wasteful, rely on luck, and the quality control is often dodgy. Still, it works pretty well for our purposes. After all, the past 500 years of science haven't been *too* bad.

Nanotechnology, the manipulation of matter at the level of billionths of a meter, promises to change all of this thrashing about when we manufacture things. We are learning to build things from the bottom up, molecule by molecule.

Many people today know that nanotechnology refers to something small, and that's accurate, but more important, humanity is learning how *nature* builds things, getting down to the scale of how cells produce new proteins, cells, and structures. The promise of nanotechnology was first articulated by physicist Richard Feynman in the 1950s in his paper "There's Plenty of Room at the Bottom." Feynman surmised that throughout industrial history we used machines to make ever-smaller copies of themselves. It takes a big factory to make smaller machine tools, which in turn can make even smaller pieces of machinery. This principle continues right down to what's called Micro Electro-Mechanical Machines, or MEMS, which are working machine parts measured in microns—a small motor the size of a dust mite, for example.

The thinking behind nanotechnology carries this thinking down to the molecular level. One day, we should be able to use tiny machines to tear apart material molecule by molecule and reorganize those molecules exactly as we want them. Theoretically, it could be possible to tear trash and toxic waste apart into their component raw materials, making it easier to recycle them. Imagine turning your trash back into its raw materials and then building something new out of it with minimal waste. When we reach the level of molecular machine, our materials could make copies of themselves, repair themselves, and assemble themselves with near-perfect quality control. The idea behind this lofty goal is that the smaller we make machinery, reducing it down to the level of molecules, the more we will be mimicking cells. Ultimately, nanotechnologists are aiming at producing "molecular assemblers" that will be able to help materials and machines make perfect copies of themselves.[1] It's not technically impossible—it's what our cells do every day—but it certainly is a paradigm shift in how we manufacture things. Instead of copying the competition, we will be copying Mother Nature.

Experts in physics and chemistry see nanotechnology not as a distinct discipline but as the next frontier in all the sciences, one that will increase our power to control our natural environment exponentially. Today, nanotech means making fabrics that reject stains; tomorrow it could mean diamonds for a dollar a pound and cancer-fighting robots in your blood. It also seems to suggest manufacturing so efficient that it could put some industries out of business. For example, what will manufacturers do when materials are programmed to assemble themselves into complex machines? How do you make money as a machinist when, let's say, car parts assemble themselves? According to some forecasts, one day we will be able to take a pile of dirt and rearrange the molecules into a couch or a home computer. How? Well, that is not quite out of the theoretical stage yet, but what is happening today is just as interesting.

From Nanomaterials to Nanomachinery

In the near term, nanotechnology will create new materials with unexpected new properties. In the long term, the sky is the limit. It is quite difficult to talk about nanotechnology without sounding a little overeager and breathless. Terms like "next industrial revolution" and "unprecedented power" are bandied about. The initial applications are much more humble, so we will start, well . . . small.

NEAR TERM

Nanotechnology really means *nanomaterials*, materials that use things measured in nanometers (one billionth of a meter). Although nanotech is envisioned to be *active* nanotech (little machines designed to replicate themselves with increasingly smaller parts), right now we are experimenting with and benefiting from materials a few nanometers in size. Let us take a look at a few things we have discovered so far.

To begin with, you are likely to hear about carbon nanotubes, or Buckminsterfullerenes (named after the similarities nanotubes share with the geodesic dome of Buckminster Fuller). Discovered by the late Nobel laureate Richard Smalley, the carbon 60 atom is a form of carbon with unusual properties because of its nanoscale structure. Stronger yet lighter than steel, sometimes a conductor, sometimes an insulator, and able to carry other molecules trapped in its cagelike structure, the nanotube is one of the key building blocks of nanotechnology. Potential applications for these smart little structures seem to have no boundaries: tiny semiconductors, energy storage, conductive composites, sensors, displays, the list goes on. Today, the applications are just starting to pile up.

Recently, researchers have been using carbon nanotubes in place of conventional carbon fibers, achieving large gains in such critical material properties as tensile strength and electrical and thermal conductivity. The Florida Advanced Center for Composite Technologies (FACCT) recently announced the discovery of "buckpaper," a paper product that is ultrathin, electrically conducting, and 10 times lighter than steel but 250 times stronger. Potential products could be ultralight aircraft, superlightweight body armor, or anything else you would like to be 250 times stronger than steel at one tenth the weight.

Researchers at the University of Illinois at Urbana-Champaign have created single-walled carbon nanotubes wrapped with DNA that can be placed inside living cells to detect trace amounts of harmful contaminants using near-infrared light. It is believed that these sensors could go a long way toward uncovering the roots of disease and give pharmaceutical developers better biomarkers, showing them when and why drugs function.

Nanotechnology researchers at the University of Texas at Dallas and at Trinity College in Dublin, Ireland, have developed nanotube fibers that are stronger and tougher than any known fiber—20 times tougher than steel and 17 times tougher than Kevlar. As you can imagine, the applications here are endless: Aerospace, automotive, and construction would all benefit from such advances. Nanotubes themselves remain prohibitively expensive at several hundred dollars a gram, but as in many industries, manufacturers are already competing to make this key material more cheaply.

On the much more usable realm, and happening today, the Nano-Tex company of Austin, Texas, produces fabrics specially designed with nano-sized particles woven into the material, which make them virtually stainproof. Eddie Bauer Nano-Tex khakis feature surface fibers of 10 to 100 nanometers. This special construction solves the problem of stains at their root; because stains are just particles that are trapped in the fabric, the Nano-Tex treatment keeps the particles from setting in, while keeping the fabric soft and comfortable.

It may sound like a prosaic application for a technology that is supposed to change the world, but the technology is still in its early years. If you happen to be a dry cleaner or a maker of laundry detergent, don't you feel bigger changes on the horizon?

LONG TERM

Here is where the wacky, disruptive ideas and, of course, lots of the interest come into play. Although today's applications of nanotechnology may seem a little mundane, it is the *theoretical* possibilities—things that may ultimately overturn economies—that are exciting people. These potential applications include:

- A device the size of a remote control that could hold all human information (as nanotech increases the density of memory exponentially)

- A space elevator—nanomaterials, stronger than steel but too cheap to care about, used to make a structure so tall we can use it to launch vehicles into space inexpensively, safely, and easily

- "Nanorobots" programmed to function as immune systems by tracking cancer cells, viruses, or bacteria

These possibilities are based on the idea that through nano-technology we will be able to disassemble most things and reassemble them precisely as we want them to be. We will turn old bricks into diamonds. Nanobots will take landfills and build new cities out of them. The sky will be the limit. Mind you, *nobody* has any practical idea of how this will come to be. Theoretically, there does not appear to be anything that would make this impossible. The first attempts at flight were hundreds of years ago; eventually we landed on the moon. The first mechanical computer was created in the nineteenth century; it was not until the transistor was invented that things really took off. The more outlandish forecasts about nanotechnology may take time, but there is no reason to count them out just yet. Several companies, such as Zyvex and Nanosys, are developing the building blocks—such as tools for nanotech research and carbon nanotubes for use in manufacturing—of a nanotechnology industry. Nanotechnology may well be a revolution, but as with so many technological revolutions, it may take time to take hold.

The Downside and Upside of Nanotechnology: Scenarios

Speculation about the future of nanotechnology is not always rosy. Several scenarios of potential threats to humans if we can't keep the technology in check have been advanced.

One of the foundations of nanotechnology is that designers can make it self-replicate, not unlike the way a cell does. The term "grey goo," refers to a scenario in which certain nanomaterials are programmed to use any substance with which it comes into contact as fuel for its self-replication. Thus, for example, if the grey goo comes into contact with a chair, it dissolves the chair and rearranges the atoms into more grey goo.

One nanotechnology researcher quipped that this scenario is about as likely as a car running out of gas and then eating everything in sight in search of new sources of fuel. Although nanotechnology may have other negative consequences, government agencies are focused primarily on a link between inhaling nano-sized particles and cancer. The real nightmare scenarios affect those responsible for industries, such as steel, if nanoplastics truly are stronger than sheet steel.

Although some wonder about a potential apocalypse resulting from nanotechnology, others see nanotech as a panacea that will bring us the power to transcend pollution, poverty, even death. Ray Kurzweil, inventor, technologist, and author of *The Age of Spiritual Machines*, recently wrote a book entitled *The Singularity Is Near: When Humans Transcend Biology*. In it he posits that technologies are advancing so rapidly, overlapping each other, that we are about to go beyond biology and transcend what it means to be human. Kurzweil asserts that nanotechnology will intersect with biotechnology, curing disease, enhancing our abilities, and possibly letting us live forever. In his many essays, he states that "post-humans" are the next phase of human evolution, possibly persons of unprecedented physical, intellectual, and psychological ability, self-programming and self-defining, and potentially immortal.[2]

I have no proof that these things will or won't happen one day, but Kurzweil, who is in his mid-fifties, believes we will see significant life extension in the next 40 or so years. This is exciting, but as a professional futurist, I am bothered that I have never read anything else like it written by biotechnology experts, or by chemists and physicists who study nanotechnology. Anything is possible given enough time, but as a responsible futurist, I demand to see people who know more than I do say something is likely before I base any recommendations on it.

Here's hoping that in 100 years I discover I was wrong as I enjoy a pollution-free, disease-free, poverty-free world, thanks to nanotech!

CHECKLIST: Driving the Future of Nanotechnologies

✔ We are learning to manipulate matter at the level of billionths of a meter, which may open all sorts of new possibilities.

✔ We are learning to build materials molecule by molecule, from the "bottom up," which is not unlike the way nature creates new materials in our cells.

✔ Nanotechnology is allowing researchers to make materials with custom properties: light, strong, adhesive, flexible, and so on.

✔ Be on the lookout for carbon nanotubes, which are lighter and stronger than steel and good conductors of electricity.

✔ Some people think that nanotech could unleash tremendous power, curing disease and ending poverty. Others see the potential for environmental disaster. (Most people looking at new research in materials science don't see either of those extreme scenarios just yet).

IMPLICATIONS: Nanotech

1. *Small business, this may not involve you for a while.* Nanotechnology is fascinating and will result in all kinds of important developments. But small-business owners and leaders may not feel any change for some time. Still, keep your head up and continue to follow the new

technologies that come from nanotech—a threat or opportunity may pop up faster than you expect!

2. *Large business, your R&D may depend on nanotech.* Ten years ago, if you mentioned "nanotechnology" they thought you watched too many episodes of *Star Trek*. Five years ago, corporations were only expressing a passing interest. Today, some materials companies and pharmaceutical manufacturers are cashing in on their investments in nanotech. If you're a technology-driven company, and you don't at least have an eye on this subject, you may be missing the boat. Nanotech will likely make big promises that will look a little overblown for the first few years. But when they pay off, the changes will be serious. Monitor this one closely.

CHAPTER FOURTEEN

media and communications

six billion channels for six billion people

R adio. Television. The Food Network. Canal +. The NASCAR Channel. Telemundo. The Weather Channel. CNN. Comedy Central. Sky Sports. The Internet. Newspapers. Print magazines. Online magazines. Podcasts. Blogs. Cell phone videocasts. Blackberries. CRACKberries.

AARGH! The chatter never stops! In the gym, rows of televisions line the available space in front of cardio equipment. In bars and airports, television is never far. Coffee shops have wireless connections. Cell phones can download e-mail, surf the Web, and even watch video downloads. No matter where you go, anywhere more than 100 people congregate you are *connected*.

As information and communications technology flourished, the ability to broadcast an endless stream of audio, video, and text anywhere and everywhere on earth expanded exponentially. As devices shrink in size and increase in power, we have developed the ability to send messages everywhere, whether in the form of phone calls or television shows. From the moment you are born, you are bathed in electronic communications.

Three major trends will change how media affects us in the future. First, our electronic devices are merging the different types of media into one digital mix. Second, corporate consolidation of media is reducing the number of people who control media and own the intellectual property rights of our cultural output. Third, the arms race of competing media messages is creating a generation of kids who don't take anything that comes from the media as gospel. Amid all the noise, simple credibility may be the most valuable commodity in the world.

Digital Devices: Blurring Media Lines

As we have seen with record companies, innovations in media and communications are occurring rapidly. The number-one driver of this is the power of information technology, governed by Moore's Law (see Chapter 9). Every year, the devices to create, communicate, and play digital media get smaller and more powerful. A few years ago, you could carry a cell phone, a computer, and a portable video player to be able to make phone calls, send and receive e-mails, and view movies. Today, a Treo portable office will do all of that in one device. "Media" are converging into one continuous, interactive, digital stream of information.

By 2020, multimedia will be the rule, not the exception. People will receive data through a variety of devices that can deliver both pictures (still images and videos) and audio. When the Internet is fast enough to have good-quality streaming video, will we still have TVs? The point is, it won't matter what device plays it, as long as it's digital.

Also, consider the havoc to the media industry if nanotechnology fulfills its promise to provide exponentially more digital storage. With a few million gigabytes of storage, it will be possible to capture thousands of hours of movies and *years'* worth of music. If that happens, the movie industry is in for the same trouble as the music industry was. Even though we now have iTunes, the music industry isn't on easy street yet. Today, a nice 200-GB hard drive can store 50,000 songs using the MP3 format. As memory density increases, you will be able to have millions of songs.

What will we do when we can keep 10 years' worth of movies and music on our person at all times? Will we get anything done? Will boredom be a thing of the past? How will kids pay attention in class if they can take these devices to school with them? With digital media, we will soon be the most entertained people in history, for good or ill.

Still, there is one old-school technology—the book—that seems to hang on despite rapid advances in electronics. Predictions of the demise of the book seem to have been greatly exaggerated. People keep trying to pinpoint when the book will be history. The e-book, first developed in the late 1990s, was thought to be a potential threat to the printed book. Because you are likely reading a hard copy of this book, apparently that forecast was a bit premature. The death of the book was predicated on faulty assumptions, principally that books were low tech and would give way to high-tech sources of information like palmtop computers. Actually, books are highly refined technologies, but they are also pretty simple. They get information to the consumer in a durable, reliable format that doesn't break down much, except maybe when soaked in liquid. It's true—books don't like coffee, but your laptop likes coffee even less.

People like books. The laptop is a terrible technology to curl up with in bed. The book-buying public was reared on books as its primary source of information. People remember books from childhood, from school, from college term papers. People relate to the dusty smell they associate with erudition that emanates from the stacks in the local library. Books carry real emotional weight, which is why the prediction of their replacement by newer technologies was premature.

The times they are a' changing. The Millennial generation—today's teenagers—communicate with each other through instant messaging, cell phone text messaging, and e-mail. They research academic papers on the Internet, never seeing hard copy of the data they are searching. Broadband Internet is piped into dorm rooms these days, so the countless hours spent online may not even take place in a library. As a result, young people today are forming attitudes about how they receive data that are different from any other generation's. Millennials expect data to be easy to locate, searchable, and free. Books fail on all three counts.

Why does this matter? Because one of the best things about digital media is that it can be customized by the user, cut up, and used in other forms. An IBM study, "The End of TV as We Know It," shows that users of media want to use content for their own purposes.[1] Teachers often want to create new media. Consumers want to customize data for their own needs. According to IBM, instead of clamping down on rights to this information, open it up to your cherished customers. They will make new types of media out of it and become even more loyal to your products.

Books, to bridge the gap posed by their lack of functionality in the eyes of the Millennial generation, will have to find new ways to make their technology relevant to these demanding new consumers. Future capabilities of IT will make it cheap and feasible to include with every book a memory chip that can download the book directly to your computer in whatever the .pdf software format of 2020 will be. In this fashion, a consumer could instantly search his or her newly purchased information. We are seeing this technology used in book marketing today. A recent compendium of *New Yorker* cartoons comes with a CD-ROM that includes all 63,000 drawings that appeared in its pages over the years. I'm not giving up my printed copies of books, but if books also go digital, I will have the best of both worlds.

Media Consolidation and the Future of Intellectual Property

Who runs the media is changing almost as quickly as the way in which it arrives to you. A funny thing happened when Time and Warner Brothers merged. The combined collection of trademarks, copyrights, and pure cultural icons owned by the company is astonishing. This list contains just a few of the things it owns: CNN, Time, Scooby Doo, HBO, Bugs Bunny, Superman . . . thousands of movies, TV channels, and magazines. The company seems to own a good deal of the pop culture of the last 100 years. Combine this collection with all the other mergers and consolidation in the media industry—Sony, Bertelsmann, Fox, and Disney—and you see that, increasingly, the information people receive is controlled by fewer entities, all of which are consolidating their catalogs of intellectual property.

Meanwhile, advertisers are so hungry to "build a brand" that this has become a catchphrase, an indication of its importance. In addition, companies are claiming trademarks and service marks on very simple English sentences. Now protected by international copyright laws are:

○ "It's all good." (Buick)

○ "Make it better." (Timberland)

○ "That was easy." (Staples)

Maybe I am overreacting, but are we rapidly approaching a world in which a simple conversation in the English language could subject both participants to lawsuits from major corporations?

"Hi.® How are you today?™"

"Be careful.© We may be in contravention of service copyrights by talking."

"That's all right.™ I'll take my chances."

As it stands, it looks like language will be owned by a few corporations bent on collecting official rights to a large number of cultural concepts, stories, characters, and images, and that the future could be stifled by the control of public dialogue.

Blogs vs. the Dreaded Mainstream Media

Giant media conglomerates haven't taken over the world *quite* yet. As corporate media has consolidated, there has been stiff competition from individuals armed with powerful computer software who are creating their own publications, music, and films. The age of the blogger is here.

In the early days of the Internet, Web pages were a bit of a mystery to most people. To display content, you needed some understanding of the simple HTML language, a "Web host" whose server would house your data for the world to see, and knowledge of how to upload what you created so that it functioned for the average viewer. Not exactly as complex as delicate heart surgery, but not obvious either. As the price of Web hosting began to drop and many companies designed simple software to let anybody upload simple content to the Web, the barrier to entry dropped for those wishing to see their ideas on their very own Web page. Soon, the number of "web logs" (eventually shortened to "blogs") exploded. Would-be authors and journalists who wanted millions to have the opportunity to read their thoughts were emancipated from editors; long delays in the book-publishing cycle; and, most important, expense.

Soon, it was trumpeted everywhere that the old media was dead—Long Live the New Media! People, according to the myth, were tired of "MSM" (mainstream media) and hungered for "spin-free" data from a populist perspective. Of course, especially on sites dedicated to world events, blogs link primarily to articles and video from major media outlets to sculpt their discussions: "*Can you believe what the* Wall Street Journal *editorial page has to say—check this link!*" Clearly, the need exists for a balance between professional journalists and writers putting in the time to properly research topics and the raw, exhilarating freedom of uploading unvetted ideas without regard to advertisers or book sales.

The popularity of blogs cannot be underestimated, however, because it is an indication of a larger trend: people's skepticism about information that comes from official sources. The Pentagon has approximately 800 press agents and the federal government employs thousands of media professionals. Major companies and even religious organizations are increasingly "media savvy." The average person is acutely aware of spin and that our institutions have muscled apparatuses designed to keep us thinking about their version of events. Thus, official communications are becoming as suspect and lacking in credibility as any other form of information.

Blogs were the first to offer a kaleidoscopic filter on world events—any filter you want to apply is somewhere on the Internet. Why listen to the White House tell you its spin on reality when you can get an interesting version from the Socialist Party, right-wing revolutionaries, punk musicians, feminists, North Korean worshippers of Kim Il-Sung, etc.?

From the White House to your house, media is so ubiquitous that it will ultimately be judged on sincerity and timeliness—that is, Is this true, and do I get it when it's fresh? That is the thing about data, especially in a knowledge-driven economy: Information is like a nice French baguette, not a Twinkie. It has no preservatives, no shelf life, and grows stale rather quickly—not that tasty the following day and worthless the day after.

The Future of Advertising

There is a group of people deeply concerned about the relative skepticism toward the media. Advertisers count on you watching programs and trusting, at least to some degree, what their commercials say. With the new technologies and changing attitudes of young people, this is not easy.

As all of these devices deliver "media content," there has been a solid increase in the number of advertising messages we receive every day. Radio and TV have been around for a long time, but now there are ads on search engines, on Web pages, speeding by in cabs, appearing in video games, on our cell phones, even splattered against buildings in cities. Given the trends in small, dumb IT, we will see even more simple devices that will be cheap and that have only one purpose—to advertise to us. We will have more media in strange places, such as little screens in the grocery aisles, and eventually even on the packaging. As we walk down the grocery aisle, the packaging will call out with little videos and sound clips. Wherever you go in the industrialized environment, some form of content will bombard you, be it entertainment, advertising, or marketing.

This is taking our already fractured attention span and dicing it ever more finely. The messages are wearing off in terms of effectiveness, too. Skeptical kids of today and tomorrow will have survived every kind of marketing message possible and will continue to filter all but the most relevant and reliable. Increasingly, however, this kind of marketing shtick will be beamed right to our person as PDAs and phones get more bandwidth. This technology will make PR spin harder, not easier; people's attention spans are beginning to shut down, and, therefore, attention isn't the currency of today's marketing; it is credibility. Every member of industrialized society will have grown up having seen and heard thousands of claims that were untrue, be they in overspun media stories or in the millionth marketing campaign to turn some product or person into a "brand."

CREDIBILITY MARKETING

Selling in a world where even kids know BS when they read it is hard work.

There is clearly a backlash to all the promotion and spin happening due to the expansion of the public relations and marketing fields. Consider a recent trend in beer advertising by filmmakers such as Errol Morris to sell beer without the slightest bit of hype or sex appeal. The ad campaign, which featured more than two dozen spots, extolled the virtue of this American-made, low-brow macrobrew, extolling men to be men, take their time, not get caught up in the hype. Why was this effective? Evidently, marketers such as Miller have discovered through research that the younger demographics are in fact much more resistant to media spin than their older counterparts are. The marketers conclude that because people between the ages of 18 and 25 have been exposed to a never-ending stream of commercials, cobranding, buzz marketing, and other tools of the marketing trade they have developed a resistance to messages that are hyperbolic, overblown, or dishonest. This generation wants a straight answer and has seen enough spin to know the difference.

Never in history has there been this much 24/7 media to soak the human psyche. This is a particular challenge for the marketer of the future. How can you establish a trusted brand when there are 1,000 existing brands and 100,000 new brands using every media channel—from wearable computer ads beamed directly to customers, to video screens, radio, or any Internet connection. To get a little peace, a little privacy, that person has to develop a filter or end up becoming frazzled.

It looks like honesty may be the best policy—or at least a reasonable facsimile of honesty. Bombast will decrease in potency over time.

NANOMARKETING

Consumers are finding new ways of filtering out information that they don't specifically want. New technologies such as spam filters and "dashboards" allow people to view only the knowledge or information they need or want. This could be the first set of technologies specifically designed to defeat the modern marketing industry. The more people know exactly what they want to see, whether through their Web portal or on their televisions by using a TiVo, the more they will filter out "garbage" like unwanted advertisements. For the advertiser, the future is daunting.

My question to all media professionals, therefore, is, How are you reaching the bagpipers of the world? I'll bet, unless your name is Alastair MacDougal and you are wearing a kilt as you read this, that this question is not foremost on your mind. Let me explain.

Before I became a futurist, I was a professional musician touring on the Scottish and Irish music circuit. In fact, I occupied an ultratiny niche as a bass player accompanying highland bagpipes. Most of the concerts took place at Scottish Highland Games on the east coast of the United States, where thousands would gather at places like Loon Mountain; New Hampshire; and Bethlehem, Pennsylvania. There, folks drove from hours away to dress in kilts, watch traditional Scottish sports such as caber tossing and sheepherding, suffer the culinary challenge of haggis, and listen to bagpipes. Musicians plied their wares, CDs, and T-shirts.

The fans were voracious. People would buy CDs without ever having heard our band perform. What seemed odd and perhaps out of all perspective was that we were, to these fans, stars. Fan websites sprang up and hundreds traveled all summer around the East Coast to see their favorite bands perform.

Perhaps there is a lesson in this. Maybe the way forward is not through mass marketing but with micromarketing, which brings me back to my question: How do you reach the bagpipers of the world? These people are passionate about their hobby and are clamoring for information about which products to buy. They actually want those ads. Digital technology, because of its interactive nature, can leverage this desire. People can, through technology, receive only advertisements that interest them.

As my good friend and sports fanatic Caleb Patten said, "I will give you all my personal information about my buying habits if you give me a device to make sure I never have to see a tampon commercial again." Makes sense to me. Kids won't have to see advertisements for "boring adult shows." Recovering alcoholics won't have to see beer commercials. Women will get TV commercials announcing the new sale in the women's department instead of sitting through the men's deodorant commercial.

The future, with its overload of digital information beamed to us constantly, can be tamed if we are allowed control over the content. It could be six billion channels for six billion people.

CHECKLIST: Driving the Future of Media and Communications

    ✔ Digital devices are mixing "media" into one stream of information, be it text, audio, or video.

    ✔ One of the killer apps for media is that it can be customized by the consumer—cut up and "remixed" to create new content.

    ✔ Digital is great, but it is not the only game in town. Books are still doing well because there is something appealing about the medium of paper.

    ✔ Media companies are merging into giant conglomerates that own an increasing number of copyrights and control what we see and hear.

    ✔ As big as corporate media has become, blogs and podcasts are manifestations of a backlash, offering people the opportunity to make their individual voices heard.

    ✔ The cacophony of advertising and PR is making younger generations quite skeptical of advertising and media in general, forcing advertisers to use new tactics.

    ✔ As technology lets us custom order what media reaches our eyes, the future will be in *micromedia* as it begins to replace mass media for certain forms of advertising. We'll have a world where everybody is famous—at least to *fifteen people.*

IMPLICATIONS: Media

1. *You had better be honest and polite to advertise to the next generation.* Younger generations have been bombarded with so many ads from the mass media they have learned to tune it all out. To be heard, you'll need more than blanket advertising campaigns. You'll need to create relationships with those to whom you wish to advertise. You may need their permission to reach them as spam filters expand to a variety of devices. And since Generation Y has been raised with the most advertising of any generation in history, sincerity and directness may be the only way to reach a group weaned on cynicism.

2. *Don't hog your ideas—get used to a world of free-flowing intellectual property.* The trend in both hardware and software is for consumers to use media for "remixes" and "mashups," adding their own content right in between the audio or video they download. If your company is squeamish about consumers taking your intellectual property and using it without permission, think again. Remember how MP3s changed how young people saw who owned music. This will be happening with movies, books, TV shows, and other media, not to mention your advertising campaigns. Plan your legal strategy well in advance—the media business of tomorrow may not function well if it depends on today's 300-year-old copyright laws.

3. *If you're a small company—look sharp!* Today, you can tell the difference between fancy Manhattan advertising and small-town, homemade ads for the hometown paper. As technology advances, and tomorrow's generation knows computers natively, professional-looking media will be less costly to achieve. More, smaller players will achieve that slick media presence.

CHAPTER FIFTEEN

ecology and sustainability

growth can be good

The future offers some incredible opportunities. We are making tremendous advances in understanding disease, customizing biology to our specifications, sharing knowledge as never before, even learning a few tricks from Mother Nature to make the things we want. If we finally get the hang of cheap solar energy, things will really be looking good.

A problem, however, overshadows this progress. It appears that human industry, as it is today, reduces the ability of future generations to live on this planet. There are a variety of environmental problems: air pollution, extermination of species, destruction of the rain forest, and accumulation of chemical pollutants in the soil and water, among others. The two biggest and potentially most dangerous issues are global warming and the diminishment of freshwater tables. Global warming seems especially threatening. Cockroaches might thrive in a wide range of circumstances, but humans require certain foods and temperatures to sustain the species. It is unlikely we would do well in sustained 130-degree heat accompanied by worldwide floods.

Incidentally, it is worth mentioning that our ability to colonize space is rudimentary at best. We went to the moon a few times, but we can't live there. For now, at least, we are going to have to do the best we can with this planet.

One of the main problems of warning people of impending environmental disaster is that they have heard this before. Forty years ago—perhaps even longer—we were told, "All our industrial success takes a wretched toll on the planet." Despite the warnings, we have failed to produce an alternative, more sustainable system. To prove my point, let me try the traditional method one last time.

You there, Ms. Business Leader. You too, Mr. Consumer. You are killing the planet. Now, cut it out!

No? Well, it was worth a try. One thing is clear, warnings are not enough. Environmentalism has done wonders to discourage industries from polluting recklessly, but past methods haven't taken us far enough. Actually, the business community is aware of this problem, and there is a growing movement to reconcile industry and ecology. It is called *sustainability*, and it encompasses the ideas of making money, protecting the environment, and protecting people all at once. As might be expected, business has discovered that accomplishing these three goals is tricky, but if we succeed at transforming our industries in this way, we will improve the lives of future generations. This may be the largest, most important challenge we face.

The High Environmental Price of Success

We humans are a successful bunch. If ecologists were to describe the human species as they do any other species, they would say we were doing fantastically well. So well that we have expanded to six billion from a few hundred million about 1,000 years ago, and the numbers seem very likely to increase. We not only adapt well to our environment; we are now able to alter that environment to suit our needs.

Hence the problem: There is more than a sneaking suspicion among many that we are wrecking the world with the way we live. Science and technology have given us power on a global scale and now we are affecting the very life-support system that sustains us. People have talked about these problems for more than a century. Before that time, industrial activity was not powerful enough or widespread enough to affect the entire planet, and so human beings expanded to all corners of the earth and continued innovating to increase their efficiency and power. Today that power has increased to the level where we are taxing the earth's ability to sustain us.

The human effects on different ecosystems around the world vary; among them are erosion of topsoil, poor air and water quality, and loss of plantlife and wildlife. The two greatest environmental problems, however, are global warming and a diminishing supply of freshwater. Climatologists have concluded that global warming is more and more obviously the result of human activity. Some industrial and political interests attempt to turn the discussion of global warming into a debate about whether it is really occurring, but this is not a serious debate. The only questions are: How fast is it happening? Is it reversible? and, How bad could the damage be?

The scenarios for global warming, caused unquestionably from carbon released by the use of fossil fuels, are dire. Rising sea levels could swamp coastal cities. Crops won't grow in places where they have in the past. For example, corn might not grow in Iowa's new climate, but it could in northern Quebec, where the yield might be much less. Climatologists say we can anticipate more and bigger storms, not to mention droughts, floods—everything except plagues of locusts and rivers of blood. Not every place has polluted air or dirty water, but if the climate shifts irreversibly, all of us will feel the effects.

The second major threat is that the water tables are falling on all continents. According to the United Nations, more than two billion people could be living in water-scarce areas by 2050.[1] Consider that Israel, Jordan, and Syria all share the same freshwater aquifer. Although the world focuses on religion and other geopolitical issues as the causes of insecurity in the Middle East, imagine the tension that could arise when they run out of freshwater.

It is important to remember that a relatively small proportion of the population is creating most of the environmental impact. According to some estimates, the United States has four percent of the world's population but consumes 25 percent of the world's energy as well as disproportionate amounts of other resources.[2] Moreover, in exporting the American culture of consumption, the developing world is following our example. China is adding three million cars to the earth's roads every year. Both India and China, with more than one billion residents each, are developing rapidly. Studies show that the first two things people do when their incomes rise above the poverty level are add more meat to their diets and buy cars. Groundwater pollution from factory farms and increasing fossil fuel consumption will further strain an already taxed ecosystem when China and India adopt American consumption habits.

Simply telling everyone that consumption is bad is not the solution. The future is not some massive "return to the land" where everyone camps out in tents and rides bicycles. It will not work. That is not what people want. For example, somewhere, right now there is a man in Africa, Malaysia, or El Salvador who would love a house with proper insulation, plumbing, and central air-conditioning. When he gets sick, he wants to go to a hospital stocked with medical plastics, high-tech equipment, and modern pharmaceuticals.

In short, he wants material things. They say money can't buy happiness and the best things in life are free. Maybe so, but billions of people around the world think—correctly—that refrigerated food would prevent dysentery, and *that's* priceless. Thus, our factories continue to produce material goods as fast as possible, and because the laws of microeconomics are no more likely to change than the laws of physics, there is no reason for this trend to change.

Thus, two things remain true in the sustainability debate. First, people will continue to demand material goods because those medical plastics and refrigerators keep our babies and adults from dying. Second, we are warming the atmosphere, running out of freshwater around our cities, and polluting the air to the point of an epidemic of asthma. What remains for future generations is to reconcile these debates. Industry is good, and here to stay, but we need stable climate patterns, freshwater, and clean air.

Poverty and the Environment

Poverty is no better than industrialization for the environment. As bad a rap as industrialized nations get for causing pollution through overconsumption, impoverished people are often forced to make choices that have a deleterious effect on the land, water, and air around them. It is not a coincidence that the world's poorest economies—Haiti, Afghanistan, and Uganda—also have the world's worst ecosystems.

As much as factory farming can pollute water systems with phosphorus and runoff pesticides, subsistence agriculture decimates topsoil, encroaches on wildlife, and pollutes water. Subsistence farming practiced by the poor takes significantly more land and input to produce the same amount of food as industrialized agriculture. If for no other reason than food production, the answer is not for the world to deindustrialize.

Without question, our industrial activity is the primary culprit in the stress on the planet's ecosystems, but that activity is part of an increasingly complex global economic environment. We rely on advanced technologies to sustain our way of life, and, despite what some environmentalists may think, achieving a sustainable world is not just a case of some bad actors "stopping" their acts of malfeasance.

Changing the Debate from "Environmentalism" to Sustainability

At least in the next 50 years, there does not appear to be a miracle fix for the key problems of sustainability. Energy forecasts show gradual replacement of fossil fuels. Sustainable design is reducing waste streams, but with developing economies, the world production of waste will not shrink. Continued expansion of humans into rain forests will continue to threaten biodiversity. No technological innovations are on the horizon that might solve those problems. We have to change the system itself, to ensure that it provides material goods but also harmonizes with the laws of ecology.

Changing the entire global industrial system is daunting. Until recently, the debate over the environment has been between "environmentalists" and "pro-growth business interests," squared off against each other like boxers in a ring. On one side were the polluting businesses; on the other were the environmentalists for whom all growth was bad. It was a zero-sum game. You were either for the environment or for growth.

One lesson from the first 50 years of global consciousness about this issue is clear: A fistfight between environmentalists and business will not work.

Thinkers such as Paul Hawken, author of *Natural Capitalism* and *The Ecology of Commerce*, have been trying for decades to show how, in a purely theoretical sense, reducing pollution and waste reduces the inputs a manufacturer must purchase and reduces liability for the company, increasing profits. There is much anecdotal evidence of the success that comes to businesses adopting this mind-set—not only moral success, but financial profit. It takes time to aggregate such data, and now researchers all over the world are beginning to conclude that, both theoretically and practically, green business is more than a gimmick. It is, instead, a profit-making way forward.

The best, probably most quoted example of profitable green business is Interface, Inc., a giant in the office carpet business. Ray Anderson, having built a thriving business, realized that on a grander scale he was getting paid to take "lakes of petroleum," spin them into carpets that people used for a while, and watch them get thrown into landfills. Deciding to reduce his impact on the planet, Anderson overhauled the company to make the environment a key metric of success. In doing so, Interface reduced its environmental footprint by one third. It did this by redesigning processes and products, pioneering new technologies, and reducing or eliminating waste and harmful emissions. *And* it increased its profits while doing so. This is one of the best demonstrations that reducing environmental impact does not necessarily mean trading off profits.

Starbucks has gotten into the sustainable coffee business at a high profit. Other suppliers are also trading on the idea of sustainable agriculture, and there is an increased demand for those crops, which has raised prices and made environmentally sound business more profitable.

Fast-food restaurants like Chipotle not only feature giant tasty burritos for $6, but are also expanding market share by selling pork and chicken raised using sustainable agricultural practices. Not only are these meats of higher quality, winning over customers, but the manner of their production is less taxing on the environment, rejuvenating topsoil and preventing water contamination.

Since the notion of green business began, academics have been looking for economic reasons to explain why the environment and profitable business do not necessarily have to be at odds. Since 2001, Joshua Cinner, an American Ph.D. working in Australia, has been researching the ties between healthy coral reefs and healthy economics ashore. He has focused his research on the islands of Papua New Guinea and Indonesia and has concluded that wherever you find healthy, thriving ocean ecosystems you will find the most business opportunities on land. Conversely, wherever the ocean has been overfished or polluted, there are fewer jobs and opportunities to start businesses ashore. As more data of this sort comes in the easier it will be for more business managers to explain why they are transitioning to more ecologically sound business practices.

Restorative Development: Progress to Improve the Environment

Frustration over how to become sustainable has led businesses to a turning point. It seems at odds to expand a business and reduce its environmental impact. As green architect Bill McDonough once mused, "Why is it good when a child grows, but bad when a business grows?"[3] This conundrum is on the minds of many who are exploring ways in which human industry can actually improve things rather than destroy them.

One new idea that balances growth and sustainability is *revitalization*, as proposed by sustainable-development expert Storm Cunningham. According to Cunningham, every civilization goes through this process of wrecking its environment and wondering what to do next.[4] Throughout history, major civilizations have gone through three phases of development. First, we build our initial cities out of virgin materials and on undeveloped land. Second, we maintain what we have built, slowly expanding from our city center. As we run out of space and natural materials, life starts to get more difficult and systems begin to break down. Third, we enter the final phase called revitalization. This is a creative phase in which we redevelop older, degraded areas and attempt to rebuild the natural environment that supported us through the first two phases. Instead of expanding into brand-new areas, we develop city centers that have fallen into disrepair. To complement the development of the built environment, this process also includes repairing natural systems. We clean up the local water, replant forests, and set aside room for wildlife. Instead of being "pioneers," hacking out new development from the wilderness, people are forced to turn inward and look at what is already there and what they can do to improve it.

Cunningham says that this process is as old as the first cities, but today we are living in a special time. This is the first time this process must be used globally. In the past, cities would outgrow their boundaries, run out of materials and usable space, and turn inward, but the effect was local; the other side of the *planet* didn't feel it. Today, we are overfishing our oceans, burning through old-growth forest, and using freshwater faster than we can replace it—everywhere on our planet. For the first time, humanity will not have the luxury of simply starting over using virgin materials in a new place. At six billion people and counting, earth is reaching its carrying capacity insofar as brand-new construction is concerned.

Encouragingly, revitalization gives us a new way forward. It calls on people to take a systems view of development, which means you look at all development and make sure it functions—economically, environmentally, and socially. If you make sure it makes money, reduces the impact on natural systems, and improves people's lives, then development is good all the way around. This is perhaps less grandiose than "saving the planet," but it is more attainable.

Now, Make Wall Street Buy It: Accounting for Sustainability

Many businesses are committed to the idea of sustainability. Most people agree that being green, sustainable, or restorative is a good thing for business. Yet even with this consensus, a big problem remains. It is almost impossible to quantify what being green means. If you can make green business profitable, of course, it counts as far as Wall Street is concerned. But what about the "profit" that comes from *not* wrecking the environment and providing a healthy place in which people can live? There is no column on the balance sheet for that yet. When you analyze the financials of any company, it is not yet possible to see if it is sustainable. Nobody has figured out how to quantify sustainability to the point where you can *value* a company more if it is sustainable. The danger is that sustainability can become little more than a public relations exercise. Sure, the company may put out glossy press releases about its "commitment to the environment," but in the current financial system, if it wants to start burning up natural resources and declare a profit, its stock price won't suffer.

The challenge for us as a culture is to develop a financial system that considers the future. Perhaps one day there will be a system of sustainable-development tax credits that could appear on an income statement, making financial analysts push companies to be more sustainable. It would be a grand day indeed if you could get rich from being good to people and the environment. That's a development we could be proud to leave to our children.

CHECKLIST: Driving the Future of Ecology and Sustainability

✔ With six billion humans and counting, our species is very successful, but our thirst for material goods comes at a high price to the environment.

✔ Global warming and clean water are two of the most pressing environmental problems.

✔ Traditional environmentalism is dead. An ideology that says profit, growth, and healthy ecosystems can go together has replaced it.

✔ Some businesses are discovering that reducing waste and pollution can increase profitability, reduce risk, and increase shareholder value.

✔ It is normal for civilizations to reach a point where they are depleting virgin natural resources and need to restore their natural environment. What is different today is that they have to do it on a planetary level.

✔ Development can be beneficial as long as it repairs broken natural systems, improves people's lives, and makes economic sense.

✔ The challenge lies in finding a way for business to account for sustainability, so that Wall Street will value sustainable companies more than those that profit in the short term while straining people and the environment in the long term.

IMPLICATIONS: Sustainability

1. *Think about how to make your growth improve society and the ecological systems that support us all.* This isn't your grandfather's environmentalism. Industry today isn't just about hoping the government doesn't regulate you out of business, or having everybody move back into tents. Looking at the success of people like Ray Anderson at Interface, and some of the new data about green business, you can design your facilities and manufacturing processes to

harmonize with nature and improve profit. People, planet, profit—these are tricky to balance, but there are some good examples show that these things aren't mutually exclusive. You can do well by doing good. Enviro-optimism is cool again.

2. *Determine how to measure what you do in terms of money, social responsibility, and ecological impact.* The first step in making things better for people, ecology, and the bottom line is measuring all three of these things. Sure, you look at the revenue and profit each quarter, but think about how your processes affect people, locally and globally. Can you put numbers on jobs created, families sustained, rising real estate prices, educations financed? Think about your impact on ecological systems. Do you regularly measure the amount of recycling inputs you use? What about resources saved through innovative processes? You can't improve these things until you start measuring them.

3. *The burned-out city of yesterday is the fertile field of tomorrow's success.* Buffalo, New York. Metz, France. Swindon, England. The world is full of places that industry blessed with success and then forgot. Other places, such as Baltimore's Inner Harbor and Paris's 14th arrondissement, are taking old industrial centers and building livable, prosperous communities without expanding further into the suburbs. If you are picking a site for a new manufacturing plant or office building, consider revitalizing older, worn areas. The data show

that revitalizing old areas is often more profitable than building on Greenfield. Buy used! It will save the earth and make you more money.

where do we go from here?

You have just read about a wide-ranging group of topics that will affect the future. No matter who you are or what you do, aging populations, ecological stability, the supply of energy, and information technology are going to have an effect on your life. These fields are often linked, but none of us can possibly be an expert in them all. There is simply too much data washing over us like a tidal wave, and we cannot deal with it all, at least not at one time. This is why we must start somewhere, and do what we can.

In studying the future, the perfect is the enemy of the good. It is better to know *some* of the important things the future holds than to focus only on today.

You are perhaps wondering what to do next. You have two options. First, you can try your hand at studying the future for your company. Decide what topic is of greatest interest to you and apply the tools you have just learned to that issue. If there is one thing you take away from this book, I hope it is the realization that anybody can know more about the future. It does not require an advanced degree or an IQ of 200.

Most of the companies that are successful at understanding the future start—simply enough—by wanting to know more. Once you decide to go down this road, it really isn't hard; it's mostly reading and putting the pieces together. In your exploration, start with a systems map, collect the best available trends, and find out what the experts are forecasting. Once you have amassed all this interesting information, you and your colleagues can begin a discussion inside your company about what it all means. It truly takes only a desire to read and collect new information, and the willingness to allot enough time to discuss what it might mean. You can make a difference in your organization's thinking, whether you spend five minutes a week or make it your entire career.

You will gain another value from having read this book. You may never undertake a study of the future yourself, but you now have a guide to show you exactly what to expect should you or your company commission a professional futures study. Let's say you hire a consultant or have a group inside your company look at the future of your company. You now know that you want:

○ A broader view of the world rather than a narrow look at the future of your own company

○ Bias-free trends based on hard data

○ To understand the implications of large-scale changes that will indicate a fundamentally new world (it's nice to know about incremental changes, but it's the transformative changes you need to see with time to spare)

You are now a more informed consumer of information about the future.

Many people faced with the challenge of examining the future are content to focus on today. If you have made it this far, you aren't one of those people.

See you in the future!

NOTES

CHAPTER 2 Systems Thinking: A Superhighway to Change

1. This idea originally appeared in "Hershey's Ordered to Pay Obese Americans $135 Billion," *The Onion*, August 2, 2000, Issue 36-26. *The Onion* is a satirical online "news source." The story is funny because it is so plausible.

CHAPTER 3 Analyzing Trends: Real Change Versus Media Hype

1. Florida Museum of Natural History, "ISAF 2002 Worldwide Shark Attack Summary," viewed at http://www.flmnh.ufl.edu/fish/Sharks/Statistics/2002 attacksummary.htm.

2. Daniel Gross, "Welcome to Miller Time, Loser," *Slate*, May 2, 2005.

3. "What's Next for Beer?" *Modern Brewery Age*, 2005.

4. Richard Brandes, "BEER Growth Brands: Cheers Identifies the Fastest-Growing Beer Brands in the U.S. Market," Adams Beverage Group, 2004, viewed at www.beveragenet.net/cheers/2004/0409/0409gbrd.asp.

5. Peter V. K. Reid, "Is Beer Obsolete? No, But Brewers Have Some Work to Do," *Modern Brewery Age*, 2005.

6. "2004 Michigan State of the Brewing Industry Review," *Michigan Beer Guide*, Volume 10, Issue 85, July August 2006, viewed at http://www.michi ganbeerguide.com/news.asp?articleid=140. This article quotes directly from the Brewers Association 2004 report.

7. "What's Next for Beer?" *Modern Brewery Age*, 2005.

8. Reid, "Is Beer Obsolete?"

9. "China's Brewing Industry Gears for Expansion," AP-Foodtechnology.com, July 10, 2004, viewed at www.ap-foodtechnology.com/news/printNewsBis. asp?id=55252.

10. Ibid.

11. "What's Next for Beer?" *Modern Brewery Age*, 2005.

12. Greg Kitsock, "The Shape of Beer to Come," *All About Beer,* November 1998, viewed at www.allaboutbeer.com/features/future.html.

13. "Current Research Trends in Genomics, Proteomics and Bioinformatics, and Their Relevance to Malting Barley," Provincial Government of Alberta, Agriculture, Food and Rural Development Directorate, viewed at http://www1.agric.gov.ab.ca.

14. "Future Challenges and Opportunities for the Brewing Industry," *Journal of the Institute of Brewing,* transcript of European Brewery Convention/The Brewers of Europe Joint Session, Dublin, Ireland, May 21, 2003.

15. "What's Next for Beer?" *Modern Brewery Age,* 2005.

16. "Future Challenges and Opportunities for the Brewing Industry," *Journal of the Institute of Brewing,* transcript of European Brewery Convention/The Brewers of Europe Joint Session, Dublin, Ireland, May 21, 2003.

17. Reid, "Is Beer Obsolete?"

18. Kitsock, "The Shape of Beer to Come."

19. Ibid.

CHAPTER 4 Into the Future: Making Judgments; Evaluating Forecasts
1. "China's Brewing Industry Gears for Expansion," AP-Foodtechnology.com, July 10, 2004, viewed at www.ap-foodtechnology.com/news/printNewsBis.asp?id=55252.

2. Ibid.

3. "Current Research Trends in Genomics, Proteomics and Bioinformatics, and Their Relevance to Malting Barley," Provincial Government of Alberta, Agriculture, Food and Rural Development Directorate, viewed at http://www1.agric.gov.ab.ca.

4. Daniel Gross, "Welcome to Miller Time, Loser," *Slate,* May 2, 2005.

CHAPTER 6 Scenario Generation: Drawing a Picture of the Future
1. Private interview with Joe Coates.

CHAPTER 7 Communicating the Future—Even to the Skeptical
1. Check out Ian's thoughts about the future at http://www.btinternet.com/~ian.pearson/.

CHAPTER 8 Aging: Preparing for a New Grey World
1. Jim Maceda, "The Strain of Italy's Aging Population," *NBC News,* December 9, 2003, viewed at http://msnbc.msn.com/id/3225883/.

2. D. Dhaval, et al., "The Effects of Retirement on Physical and Mental Health Outcomes," National Bureau of Economic Research, viewed at http://www.nber.org/papers/W12123.

3. Alcohol Alert, The National Institute on Alcohol Abuse and Alcoholism, April 1998, viewed at http://pubs.niaaa.nih.gov/publications/aa40.htm.

4. "The New Retirement Survey," available at the Merrill Lynch website at http://www.ml.com/index.asp?id=7695_7696_8149_46028_46503_46635.

5. Check out sites like http://www.accessibleurope.com/ for more information.

6. J. Bretschneider and N. McCoy. "Sexual Interest and Behavior in Healthy 80 to 102-Year-Olds," *Archives of Sexual Behavior,* 14 (1988): 343–350.

7. The National Funeral Directors Association maintains a list of industry on its website at http://www.nfda.org/nfdafactsheets.php#trends.

8. Susan Raymond, "$18 Trillion to Change Hands: How Will Non-Profits Fare?" report from http://www.OnPhilanthropy.com.

9. Ibid.

10. "The Coming Demographic Deficit: How Aging Populations Will Reduce Global Savings," January 2005, McKinsey & Company report on global capital markets, available at   http://www.mckinsey.com/mgi/publications/demographics/index.asp.

11. Graham Fuller, "The Youth Factor: The New Demographics of the Middle East and the Implications for U.S. Policy," June 2003, available at http://www.brookings.edu/fp/saban/analysis/fuller20030601.htm.

CHAPTER 9 Information Technology: Falling in Price, Increasing in Power

1. Marshall Brain has many such forecasts on his website, specifically the future of robotics, but this set of forecasts came from his blog at http://marshallbrain.blogspot.com/2005/08/dream-machine-2005.html.

2. Manjeet Kripalani, "The Digital Village," *Business Week,* June 24, 2004, viewed at http://www.businessweek.com/magazine/content/04_26/b3889003.htm.

CHAPTER 10 Health Care: New Gadgets vs. Following Doctor's Orders

1. "Americans 'more ill than English,'" *BBC News,* May 2, 2006, viewed at http://news.bbc.co.uk/2/hi/health/4965034.stm.

2. Actually, sitting next to a French nutritionist on an Air France flight gave me the greatest insight, as she remarked that despite the rumors and the books on "French women not getting fat," France had the same problems, especially in children. For more, check out papers such as M. Romon, "Influence of Social Class on Time Trends in BMI Distribution in 5-year-old French Children from 1989 to 1999," *International Journal of Obesity* 29 (2005): 54–59. To see that all of Europe is nearing U.S. levels of obesity, see a paper released by Swinburn et al. for the World Health Organization at http://www.heartstats.org/datapage.asp?id=4745. Japan is in a similar situation, particularly with its young people. See the paper by Matsushita et al., "Trends in Childhood Obesity in Japan over the Last 25 Years from the National Nutrition Survey,"

Obesity Research 12 (2004): 205–214, available at http://www.obesityresearch.org/cgi/content/abstract/12/2/205.

3. Phyllis Maguire, "Colonoscopy Screening Gains Momentum, But Problems Remain," *ACP-ASIM Observer*, 2002, viewed at http://www.acponline.org/journals/news/sep02/colonoscopy.htm.

4. Malpractice laws vary state by state, but Missouri has among the most punishing laws for obstetrics, allowing OB/GYNs to be sued 23 years after the birth of the baby. See William Poe, "Malpractice Malaise: Skyrocketing Medical Malpractice Insurance Rates Are a Sickness in Need of a Cure," *St. Louis Commerce Magazine*, October 2003, viewed at http://www.stlcommerce magazine.com/archives/october2003/insurance.html.

CHAPTER 11 Biotechnology: Scratching the Surface of the Secrets of Life
1. Justin Gillis, "Bionic Growth for Biotech Crops," *Washington Post*, January 12, 2006, D01.

2. Dr. Michel Levesque of Cedars-Sinai Medical Center in Los Angeles is at the forefront of this research. His recent testimony to Congress explains his work in detail. Viewed at http://commerce.senate.gov/hearings/testimony.cfm?id=1268&wit_id=3670.

CHAPTER 12 Energy: Getting More out of Less
1. Susan Watts, "A Coal Dependent Future?" *BBC News*, March 9, 2005, viewed at http://news.bbc.co.uk/1/hi/programmes/newsnight/4330469.stm.

2. "The World in 2006," *Economist*, viewed at http://www.economist.com/the worldin/.

3. "Energy Efficiency Progress and Potential," American Council for an Energy Efficient Economy, viewed at http://www.aceee.org/energy/effact.pdf.

4. Regina McGarvey, "Strategies for Japan's Energy Policy: Progressing from the Past, Focusing on the Future," George Washington University, Washington, D.C., 2005.

5. Mark Morford, "God Loves the VW Dasher," *San Francisco Gate*, September 16, 2005, viewed at http://sfgate.com/cgi-bin/article.cgi?f=/gate/archive/2005/09/16/notes091605.DTL&nl=fix.

6. John Carey, "Giving Hybrids a Real Jolt," *BusinessWeek*, April 11, 2005, viewed at http://www.businessweek.com/magazine/content/05_15/b3928103.htm.

7. "International Energy Outlook 2006," U.S. Department of Energy, viewed at http://www.eia.doe.gov/oiaf/ieo/coal.html.

8. John Lawton, "No Shortcut to Sustainable Energy," *Spiked*, February 18, 2002.

9. See the Risø Energy Laboratory's annual reports at http://www.risoe.dk/rispubl/annual.htm.

10. From a speech given at the National Capitol Region World Future Society, Washington, D.C., "The Geopolitics of Energy: A Forward View," March 16, 2006. Go to http://www.natcapwfs.org for more information.

11. "Titania Nanotube Arrays Harness Solar Energy," *Clean Edge News*, February 6, 2006.

12. Lawton, "No Shortcut to Sustainable Energy."

13. Check out the website at http://www.usgbc.org.

CHAPTER 13 Nanotechnologies: Smaller Is Better

1. The concept of molecular assemblers and "machines with reproductive systems" is brilliantly explained by Dr. Rob Freitas and Dr. Ralph Merkle in their most recent book, *Kinematic Self-Replicating Machines*, available for free online at http://www.molecularassembler.com/KSRM.htm.

2. Check Ray Kurzweil's website at http://www.kurzweilai.net for a complete listing of his essays and white papers.

CHAPTER 14 Media and Communications: Six Billion Channels for Six Billion People

1. "The End of TV as We Know It: A Future Industry Perspective," IBM Institute for Business Value Study, March 27, 2006, viewed at http://www-935.ibm.com/services/us/index.wss/ibvstudy/imc/a1023172?cntxt=a1000062.

CHAPTER 15 Ecology and Sustainability: Growth Can Be Good

1. Ted Gordon and Jerry Glenn, "2004 State of the Future," United Nations University Press, Washington, D.C., 2004.

2. Among other sources, see the Resources and Materials Use reports from the World Resources Institute, available at http://materials.wri.org/index.cfm.

3. From a speech given at the National Press Club of Washington, D.C., by William McDonough in 2000.

4. Cunningham's theories are elaborated on his website at http://www.revitalizationinstitute.org.

INDEX

role playing, 109–110
royalties, for seeds, 187–188
Rushkoff, Douglas, 162–163
Ruys, Thony, 70

S curve trend, 59–60
scenario generation, 103–123
    alternatives, 111–113
    applying, 110–111
    for beer, 120–122
    broad scenarios, 113–115
    checklist, 122–123
    current options, 123
    details in, 107–109
    focused scenarios, 115–116
    impact/probability matrix, 116–120
    mental image, 104–110
    value of, 104
scholarly journals, 54
sciences, overlap of, 5
security, for water infrastructure, 41
sedentary lifestyles, automobiles'
    impact on, 94–95
self-replication in nanotechnology,
    216–217
sensors, for environmental quality, 159
service sector, vs. manual labor, 70–71
sex, for aging population, 148–149
shark attacks, media impact on public
    perception, 48
Shell Eco-Marathon competition, 202
*The Singularity Is Near: When Humans
    Transcend Biology*, 217
"Sit-N-Lift," 147
skepticism, about information sources,
    226
Smalley, Richard, 213
"smart appliances," 79
"smart homes," 146
"smart packaging," 32–33
Smuttynose Brewing Co., 71
society, in STEEP analysis, 28, 100
solar power, 205–206
sources of information, 51–57
    current conditions, 51–54
    Internet for, 53
    official reports, 54–57
    peer-reviewed and scholarly jour-
        nals, 54
    reliability, 53, 78
    skepticism about, 226
Soviet Union, 118, 131
spammers, 165
specialization of skills, 143

Starbucks, 241
statins, 189
Stear, Rory, 198
STEEP analysis, 28–29, 100
    for beer study, 43–44
stem cells, 193–194
Stockholm Environment Institute,
    113–114
stories, for communication, 104
strategic planning, and futurism,
    14–16
strategic thinking, dissection, 24–27
stress, on economy, from aging popu-
    lation, 138
structured thinking, 99–102
suburbs, automobiles and, 94
success, high environmental price of,
    236–238
supercomputers, 158
superconnection, 5, 87
sustainability movement, 21, 52, 235,
    239–242
    accounting in, 243–244
    checklist, 244–245
    debate, 238
    implications, 245–247
Synthroid, 180
Syria, water supply, 237
systems analysis, 24
    of water system, 35–37
systems diagram, 33
systems thinking, 23–46
    for beer industry, 42–44
    checklist, 45
    current options, 45–46
    diagramming trends, 33–40
    fun, 44–45
    identifying players, 37–38
    research on trends, 30–33
    spotting trends, 27–33
    value of, 40–41

technology, in STEEP analysis, 28,
    100
telecommunications, Nokia invest-
    ment in, 6–7
terrorism, 15
    risk to water supply, 41
theory of alternative futures, 112
"therapeutic cloning," 194
thief in future, 108–109
threats, detecting potential, 19–20
Time Warner, merger, 224
Toyota, 201